What We Evangelicals Believe

DAVID ALLAN HUBBARD

FULLER
SEMINARY PRESS
•
PASADENA, CALIFORNIA

Copies of this book are available from
FULLER SEMINARY BOOKSTORE
135 North Oakland Avenue
Pasadena, CA 91182

Published by Fuller Seminary Press
135 N. Oakland Avenue
Pasadena, CA 91182

Printed in U.S.A.

Library of Congress Catalog Card No.: 79-51622

ISBN 0-9602638-5-3

Contents

Purpose

OF FULLER THEOLOGICAL SEMINARY

Fuller Theological Seminary, embracing the Schools of Theology, Psychology and World Mission, is an evangelical, multidenominational, international and multiethnic community dedicated to the preparation of men and women for the manifold ministries of Christ and his Church. Under the authority of Scripture it seeks to fulfill its commitment to ministry through graduate education, professional development and spiritual formation. In all of its activities, including instruction, nurture, worship, service, research and publication, Fuller Theological Seminary strives for excellence in the service of Jesus Christ, under the guidance and power of the Holy Spirit, to the glory of the Father.

Introduction

The term "evangelical" is presently shrouded in controversy. This is nothing new. The range of nuances the term has borne across the centuries has often allowed its significance to be twisted into a rope for ecclesiastical tug-of-wars.

Luther and his followers first claimed the term to describe their commitment to a gospel whose truth and power Roman Catholicism had often obscured. For them, the evangelical church was that body of believers who taught and lived the evangelical doctrines of the Reformation: the authority of Scripture alone, justification by faith in the saving work of Christ, and the full priesthood of all Christians.

Anglicans use the term to describe that movement within their church that has kept closest to their Reformation roots, particularly as expressed in the Thirty-Nine Articles of the Church of England (A.D. 1571). "Evangelical," in Anglican circles worldwide, is frequently used in contrast to "High church" or "Anglo-Catholic." It describes those believers who stress evangelism and conversion as part of the church's mission, whose commitment to Christ centers more in the preaching of the gospel than in the sacraments, and who are more than cautious about proposed alliances with the Church of Rome. In the Anglican context, evangelical loyalty often shows itself in external things—such as, serving communion from a table rather than an altar, not displaying a crucifix or burning candles, and not including petitions for the dead in the formal prayers.

In most of Latin America and other parts of the Roman Catholic world, "evangelical" is virtually synonymous with Protestant. Into the world of liturgy, mass, hierarchy, religious celibacy, and adoration of the saints has come the new, fresh word of the gospel. Freedom from law and ritual, freedom from fear and superstition, freedom from uncertainty about salvation, freedom from feelings of inferiority that plagued the laity—these and other liberating energies were brought by the gospel.

For Christians in the United States, "evangelical" has had varied connotations. One of the most prominent has been the legacy from the 18th century of John Wesley and the great revivals of George Whitfield. Spiritual vitality, warm piety, concern for mission and evangelism worldwide were among their emphases.

Another American strand of evangelicalism originated in Scandinavia. There, especially in Sweden, the rigid formalism of the Lutheran Church, together with its restricting official ties with the government, provoked a response on the part of many devout believers that led to the forming of independent congregations. Frequently they met in houses where under the cloak of secrecy they sang their gospel hymns, studied their well-worn Bibles, and prayed that the revival tides which had refreshed them would inundate their land. When the opposition of the state Church grew oppressive, they sought refuge in the New World, bringing the glowing piety of their transformed faith with them. The Evangelical Covenant Church of America, The Baptist General Conference and the Evangelical Free Church are part of their legacy to our generation. Among Anabaptists like the various Mennonite communions, a similar pattern of opposition and even persecution in Holland, Germany, and Russia impelled them to migrate to North America.

"Evangelical" can also be understood against the background of the theological liberalism that grew up within the church agencies and educational institutions of many denominations at the turn of our century. "Fundamentalism" was the term generally used to describe the movement that refused to go along with the so-called modernizing of the Christian faith, often enraging the liberalism in the denominations. Fundamentalism held tenaciously to the basic doctrines of the church as expressed in the great creeds of the first four centuries and in the evangelical confessions of the Reformation era. Beyond that, it put fresh stress on biblical verities like the lostness of the human family apart from faith in Christ, the miraculous quality of our Lord's life—virgin birth, working of miracles, bodily resurrection, the substitutionary nature of his death (which was much more than a martyr's display of love and courage)—and the hope of his personal return.

For the past fifty years or so, the term "evangelical" has described those American and Canadian Christians who viewed themselves as conservative without necessarily espousing some of the more negative traits of fundamentalism: anti-intellectualism that suspects scholarship and formal learning, especially when applied to the Bible or theology; apathy toward involvement in social concern, especially where political issues are in view; separation from all association with churches that are not themselves doctrinally pure.

The National Association of Evangelicals (founded in 1942) made a concerted attempt to rally for mission and fellowship those persons, congregations, agencies and denominations who held to evangelical doctrines and who wanted to see evangelical influences deepened in the churches, the nation, and the world. The NAE and other evangelical alliances, often encouraged by the ministry of Billy Graham and his Evangelistic Association, have witnessed amazing experiences of evangelical unity. The Wesleyan, Scandinavian, Anabaptist, Reformed, Lutheran, and Pentecostal expressions of our evangelical movement have been brought together for great conclaves and strategies in the World Congress on Evangelism (Berlin, 1966), the United States Congress on Evangelism (Minneapolis, 1969), Key '73 and the significant Congress for World Evangelization (Lausanne, 1974), and "Lausanne II" (Manila, 1989).

These concerted endeavors, together with the growth of great Christian agencies like World Vision International, Young Life, Campus Crusade for Christ, Inter-Varsity Christian Fellowship (with its massive calls to mission at Urbana) have resulted in an increase in evangelical vitality, which has caught much of the nation—especially the communications media—by surprise. The winds of God's Spirit are blowing across the land with revival-like intensity. Conversion—being born-again—is table conversation in thousands of households. The word "evangelical" is more and more a part of our national parlance.

At the same time, controversy hovers over our movement. Lines of battle are being drawn up, and some Christian leaders seem to be urging us to take sides on a variety of issues.

For some, to be evangelical means to be conservative in politics and economics. Strident spokespersons seek to rally us around their political perspective and to recruit us in Christ's name to their economic views. For some of them, what we believe about American foreign policy or approaches to government spending or the fluoridation of our drinking water is almost as important as what we believe about Christ's sacrifice or the Bible's inspiration. In turn, other evangelicals have adopted more liberal political views and are seeking, often with youthful enthusiasm, to sell others on them as the best way to express a Christian commitment in the social and political arenas. Sometimes the contest has been so fierce between these two points of view that Christian ties, which ought to be stronger among us than any political differences, have been stretched to the breaking point.

Similar tensions center in our evangelical attitudes toward the charismatic movement. Some of our brothers and sisters have discovered such vitality and joy in their experiences of the Holy Spirit that they virtually insist that all Christians seek that same experience. The "full gospel" is one of their descriptions of what they have encountered. (They may not be wholly aware that such nomenclature suggests that non-charismatics have only a partial gospel.) Charismatic exuberance has sometimes been met by the cautious curiosity of fellow Christians, but the response has often been suspicious hostility: what charismatics attribute to the Holy Spirit has been explained by others as psychic illusion or satanic deception. So, some Christians say of experiences like speaking in tongues, "All evangelicals must!" while others warn, "No evangelicals should!"

Eschatology has provided another arena of controversy. Views of the millennium or the tribulation have elbowed their way into the center of our doctrinal discussions, thereby bidding to become tests by which to distinguish orthodoxy from heresy. Classical millennialists are tempted to view those who teach a pre-tribulation rapture as sectarian interlopers lately come on the theological scene, while pretribulationists sometimes brand those who disagree as being blind to the correct interpretation of prophecy and adamantly strapped to tenets of the past.

Churchmanship has been a key source of dissension. Intense feelings separate those who seek to maintain their evangelical witness as members of denominations which allow theological diversity from those who think that fellowship with persons or churches not avowedly evangelical is an intolerable compromise.

More recently, attention has been called to differences among evangelicals in the emphasis put on the inerrancy of Scripture or in the definition of inerrancy. There are some for whom a meticulous definition of inerrancy is an absolute essential for biblical faith, and there are others who feel that the focus on the details of science, geography, and history distracts us from the saving message and the spiritual teaching of Scripture.

All of these controversies—political, charismatic, eschatological, churchly, and biblical—furnish the context of this book. Without minimizing the importance of any current questions, we must not allow the evangelical label to be pre-empted by parties on any side of these issues. More importantly, we must not allow evangelical strength to be dissipated or evangelical unity to be fragmented by them.

No one item should control the evangelical agenda. And certainly no doctrine not central to the gospel should become an ultimate bone of contention among us. From our earlier brief survey of the roots of evangelicalism is a commitment to the good news that God has made salvation possible through the death and resurrection of his Son Jesus Christ and that salvation will be the experience of those who truly trust

God for it.

When we evangelicals dig in to defend our doctrines we must be sure that the issues are central:

— the eternal Trinity;

— the reality of God's revelation in creation, history, and Scripture;

— the creation of humankind in God's image and the subsequent fall through disobedience;

— The coming to earth in human flesh of God's eternal Son—born of a virgin, fully obedient to God, working miracles as signs of God's kingdom, crucified to bear our judgement and to reveal God's love, risen bodily from the dead, ascended to the Father's side;

— the work of the Holy Spirit who enables us to believe in Christ and grow in his grace;

— the formation of the church to demonstrate God's love and to carry out God's mission in worship, nurture, evangelism and justice;

— the consummation of God's kingdom in the personal return of Jesus Christ which results in the resurrection of the race, the final separation of unbelievers from God's presence and the glorification of believers as they enjoy eternal fellowship with the triune God.

These basic doctrines are the heart of evangelical faith. On them our *Statement of Faith* at Fuller Theological Seminary focuses. As the trustees and faculty of Fuller sign this Statement annually, we try to make clear our commitment to the basics of biblical faith without falling into the trap of parochialism. Our aim is to serve the larger evangelical movement in all its expressions rather than to reinforce one segment against others.

Our preamble to this Statement makes our stance clear. The ten articles of faith that follow form the basis for the 10 chapters of this book—first presented as a series of messages on the international broadcasts of "The Joyful Sound" and in the chapel services of Fuller Theological Seminary.

Special mention should be made of the help which two of my colleagues rendered in reading the manuscripts—Geoffrey W. Bromiley and Paul King Jewett. Their suggestions were perceptive enough to convince me that this would have been a much better book if either of them had written it. Thanks for the editing goes to my wife Ruth and for the typing to Janet Johns and Vera Wils, two of our Fuller coworkers.

My profound hope is that these chapters will help lift the cloud of controversy that shadows our movement and will be an encouragement to evangelical understanding, obedience, and unity. Nothing less than these should be our goal in all we do as servants who find both our freedom and our duty in the gospel of Jesus Christ.

Statement of Faith

FULLER THEOLOGICAL SEMINARY

A foundation of faith in a changing world

Doctrinally the institution stands for the fundamentals of the faith as taught in Holy Scripture and handed down by the church. Consistent with this purpose, the faculty and trustees of the Seminary acknowledge the creeds of the early church and the confessions of the Protestant communions to which they severally belong. Under God, and subject to biblical authority, they also bear concerted witness to the following articles, to which they subscribe, and which they hold to be essential to their ministry.

---

1 God has revealed himself to be the living and true God, perfect in love and righteous in all his ways; one in essence, existing eternally in the three persons of the Trinity: Father, Son and Holy Spirit.

2 God, who discloses himself through his creation, has savingly spoken in the words and events of redemptive history. This history is fulfilled in Jesus Christ, the incarnate Word, who is made known to us by the Holy Spirit in sacred Scripture.

3 Scripture is an essential part and trustworthy record of this divine self-disclosure. All the books of the Old and New Testaments, given by divine inspiration, are the written Word of God, the only infallible rule of faith and practice. They are to be interpreted according to their context and purpose and in reverent obedience to the Lord who speaks through them in living power.

4 God, by his Word and for his glory, freely created the world of nothing. He made us in his own image, as the crown of creation, that we might have fellowship with him. Tempted by Satan, we rebelled against God. Being estranged from our Maker, yet responsible to him, we became subject to divine wrath, inwardly depraved and, apart from grace, incapable of returning to God.

5 The only mediator between God and humanity is Christ Jesus our Lord, God's eternal Son, who, being conceived by the Holy Spirit and born of the Virgin Mary, fully shared and fulfilled our humanity in a life of perfect obedience. By his death in our stead, he revealed the divine love and upheld divine justice, removing our guilt and reconciling us to God. Having redeemed us from sin, the third day he rose bodily from the grave, victorious over death and the powers of darkness. He ascended into heaven where, at God's right hand, he intercedes for his people and rules as Lord over all.

6 The Holy Spirit, through the proclamation of the gospel, renews our hearts, persuading us to repent of our sins and confess Jesus as Lord. By the same Spirit we are forgiven all our sins, justified by faith alone through the merit of Christ our Savior, and granted the free gift of eternal life.

7 God graciously adopts us into his family and enables us to call him Father. As we are led by the Spirit, we grow in the knowledge of the Lord, freely keeping his commandments and endeavoring so to live in the world that all may see our good works and glorify our Father who is in heaven.

8 God, by his Word and Spirit creates the one holy catholic and apostolic church, calling sinners out of the whole human race into the fellowship of Christ's Body. By the same Word and Spirit, he guides and preserves for eternity that new, redeemed humanity, which, being formed in every culture, is spiritually one with the people of God in all ages.

9 The church is summoned by Christ to offer acceptable worship to God and to serve him by preaching the gospel and making disciples of all nations, by tending the flock through the ministry of the Word and sacraments and through daily pastoral care, by striving for social justice and by relieving human distress and need.

10 God's redemptive purposes will be consummated by the return of Christ to raise the dead, to judge all people according to the deeds done in the body, and to establish his glorious kingdom. The wicked shall be separated from God's presence, but the righteous, in glorious bodies, shall live and reign with God forever. Then shall the eager expectation of the creation be fulfilled and the whole earth shall proclaim the glory of God who makes all things new.

STATEMENT OF FAITH ARTICLE **1**

God has revealed himself to be the living and true God, perfect in love and righteous in all his ways; one in essence, existing eternally in the three persons of the Trinity: Father, Son and Holy Spirit.

SCRIPTURE

The grace of the Lord Jesus Christ
and the love of God
and the fellowship of the Holy Spirit
be with you all.

II Corinthians 13:14

Beloved, let us love one another;
for love is of God,
and he who loves is born of God and knows God.
He who does not love
does not know God; for God is love.
In this the love of God was made manifest among us,
that God sent his only Son into the world,
so that we might live through him.
In this is love,
not that we loved God
but that he loved us and sent his Son
to be the expiation for our sins.

I John 4:7-10

CHAPTER *1*

The God Whom We Worship

To speak of God is a presumptuous thing. Our words are ill-equipped to bridge the chasm between him and us. The mystery of God's ways, the grandeur of his majesty, the loftiness of his person all serve to expose the frailty of our human minds and the poverty of our human language.

Among the ten things listed in the law that we are not to do is this: "You shall not take the name of the Lord your God in vain: for the Lord will not hold him guiltless who takes his name in vain" (Deuteronomy 5:11). God's name—the expression of God's person—is literally terrible. That is, it is frightening to deal with. Its difference from all other names is overwhelming.

To forget this is easy in an age where class and status have been largely set aside. We know the intimate habits of statesmen, sportsmen, and entertainers. The auras that once surrounded them have faded;

where we look for halos we would find them tarnished. "Great people?" we ask. What is so great about them? They, like us, bleed when they are cut, eat soup with a spoon, put on their trousers one leg at a time. We handle lightly—our generation does—the names and reputations of the wealthy, the influential, the famous. This we cannot do with God.

Jesus' lesson about prayer is now more important than ever. "Hallowed be thy name" is to stand at the head of all we think to say about our God.

It is presumptuous and so dangerous to speak about God that we dare not do so without his help. Who can speak about God at all without God's speaking first? The curtain that veils him from us can only be drawn from the inner side. The pull-cord is in God's own hands.

Our speculations are to no avail. The attempts that we have made to penetrate his mysteries ricochet off the walls of the unknown and bounce their shrapnel back to cut us. Our portraits of God are painted in the dark with colors that fade on a canvas stretched to distortion. Besides that, the chair where the subject should sit is vacant. God's face is most hidden from those who think they know what he looks like.

In such situations the words, "Be still, and know that I am God" are fitting (Psalm 46:10). Only he—the God who is there, the God who is not a projection of our imaginings—can speak to our caricatures of his nature, our presumptions about his presence, our anxieties over his absence. And how he has spoken!

It is to recognize that God must speak first to us, if we are to speak intelligibly about him, that the *Statement of Faith* begins this way: "God has revealed himself to be the living and true God, ..."The wording is essential. It does little good for us to say, "We feel that there is a living and true God," as though our belief were a matter of sentiment. Or to affirm, "We have discovered a true and living God," as if our Christian commitment were our own invention.

Whatever we can say about our evangelical faith must be said in response to what God has told and shown us. Otherwise we can never break through our own experience; we can never surmount our own limitations. Theology—what we believe about God—can never move beyond private opinion, personal hunch, individual intuition or group consensus, unless God takes the lead in revelation. Theology will be nothing but religious anthropology, a study of human conviction about religion, wherever the phrase "God has revealed himself to be..." does not stand at the beginning of our creeds.

Our humanity is too weak, our sin too vile, for us to understand who God is and what he is like unless he tells us. Made of dust and in revolt against our Maker, we cannot understand him on our own.

But God has come to our aid and shown us the wonder of his person, the dignity of his name. On information and in words he himself has supplied by his revelation we can begin to talk about his eternal character and his triune nature. But that revelation gives us no license for presumption. In fact, it increases our humility. It labels the vessel in which we hold our understanding as earthen to the core. So affirm we must, because the God who is has spoken. But because it is God who has spoken, our affirmations are modest ones. And they can only be authentic when they are informed by his own self-affirmations. The ultimate truth and glory belong to him, not to our expressions about him.

God's eternal character

Statements about God's character are always doomed to inadequacy.

Perfection defies description; infinitude cannot be captured in the limits of grammar. We cannot say everything for two reasons: 1) we do not know everything; 2) we do not have either time or space to give a fulsome description. John's Gospel noted this problem in regard to the deeds of the Son of God: "Were every one of them to be written, I suppose that the world itself could not contain the books..." (John 21:25).

We cannot say everything, true. But there are a few things that we cannot not say. Our *Statement of Faith* has focused on them: "God has revealed himself to be the living and true God, perfect in love and righteous in all his ways..."

It is the living God who has revealed himself. Think of all the other gods whom our human kindred and neighbors have worshiped. Stone, clay, wood, metal, social structures, political entities, ideological abstractions they have been. No breath to give them vitality; no movement to signify their life. To them we came—we foolish creatures—and offered our adulation. Our brains made decisions that the idols were incapable of; our metabolisms sparked a life of which images were ignorant; our organs reproduced the race which in turn had to refashion the worn-out idols. Into this vast human idol-factory, which is our world, came the living Lord, exposing the follies of our lifeless worship.

Alive and life-giving-both of those terms are imbedded in the phrase "living God." God is not just living in the sense that the philodendron is that roams your kitchen window or the caterpillar that roams the philodendron. They, like us, will die. Mortality is their middle name.

The living God is beyond death's race. His life is not a temporary gift, offered and then withdrawn. Living for him means the personification of life. Jesus spoke of this unique quality like this: "For as the Father has life in himself, so he has granted the Son also to have life in himself..." (John 5:26). "Life in himself"—he was not conceived as you and I were; not spawned, hatched, or generated by the reproductive systems of the universe. Indeed, that reproductive process that preserves and enriches life as we know it is under his orders. Only he—the living God—stands beyond it and is not subject to it. He is the life from which all else that lives derives its life.

It is the true God that has revealed himself. And what a necessary revelation! Our propensity is to falseness, especially when it comes to religion. Left to our own devices we have built pyramids, sculpted parthenons, composed symphonies, and analyzed the chemistry of Mars. Our technological skills, our esthetic judgements, our scientific calculations have a quality of distinction about them. The same cannot be said about our self-made notions of God. Our sin has led us to fabricate lies about him. "Lies" is one of the words biblical writers used to describe our human idols.

Only of the God of revelation can the word "true" be accurately used. He is dependable; he will not lead us astray. All he claims to be he is. Of no other god can that be said.

It is the loving God who has revealed himself. And only his revelation would tell us that. Struggle, competition, hostility mark so much of life from the bush of East Africa to the streets of San Francisco. On the basis of what we are and what we see, we could easily gain the impression that anger, not love, stood at the heart of the universe. Yet something within tells us that hatred cannot be what life is about. And when God demonstrates his love in the care for his people and the coming of his Son, we say, "That is it. Love, not hatred, is the key to our existence." No word captures God's disposition toward us better than the word love—that constant concern for and loyalty towards us and toward what is good for us.

It is the righteous God who has revealed himself. We often think that righteous means not to do wrong things. Of course, that definition would apply to God. But much more, righteous means "set to do right things." God's righteousness is close kin to his love. It describes the way he works to bring salvation, to do wonderful deeds on behalf of those who belong to him. For God to help the people who have trusted him and to whom he has pledged himself is right.

God's righteousness is not the meticulous observing of a checklist of do's and don'ts. It is his relentless commitment to see his people through to salvation, to accomplish his high and holy purposes in human history.

God's triune nature

What the Bible teaches about God and what the Fuller Statement seeks succinctly to summarize we could never have guessed: God is "one in essence, existing eternally in the three persons of the Trinity: Father, Son and Holy Spirit."

God has revealed himself to be one in essence. At the heart of the universe is unity—not several elements warring for supremacy, not many forces fighting for predominance, not a pantheon vying for control. One God, Lord of all life, has shown himself in human history and announced his sovereignty.

Because he is one, his claim on us is total. There are no areas of life where anyone else is in charge; there are no regions of the universe, black holes and beyond, where God himself is not in charge. He needs no passport in his travels because he knows no foreign territory; he checks no administrative chart because he has no colleagues with whom to share authority.

God has revealed himself to be three in personhood. The term person gives us problems when we speak of the holy Trinity, because person to us suggests independent, individual existence, separate bodily features and the like. None of that applies to God. What we mean by person is that there is an eternal reality to the distinction within God just as there is to his unity. Jesus the Son is more than just the form that God took when he came to earth. God the Spirit is more than just the means God used to establish his church at Pentecost.

There are many ways of looking at the mystery of the Trinity and trying to fathom its significance for us. Will it help us to connect the Trinity with what God has shown us about his love and righteousness?

If God is love to its perfection, does not the triune nature give opportunity for the expression of love from all eternity? Before the world is, before the man and the woman walk with God in the garden, God is love. And that love is expressed eternally among the persons of the Trinity.

And what about righteousness? It means the ability and the willingness to maintain right relationships. God did not begin to do this only when Adam, Noah, and Abraham strode onto the stage. Eternally, relationship has been part of who he is—Father, Son, and Holy Spirit.

In the Trinity are found love and righteousness in their purest form—unfettered by our limitations, unsullied by our sin. The love and righteousness that God has revealed in our history had an eternity of practice behind them before they even broke into our darkened lives.

All that we have said about God we know only because of his revelation. Indispensable information this is, but it is also inescapable encounter. God's revelation of himself is not only a message; it is a meeting.

Our response must be much more than "That's interesting. I had never really seen that before." God has shown himself to us, and it is an off-with-the-shoes, down-on-the-knees, flat-on the face, up-to-the work confrontation.

God's character has broken in upon us to set the style of our lives in love and righteousness. God's nature—one God; yet Father, Son, and Spirit—has brightened our lives to illuminate our service. What the triune God has called us to be—loving and righteous—he is committed to make us be.

It is both presumptuous and dangerous to speak about God. Only one thing is more presumptuous and dangerous—not to speak about him when he has spoken so clearly to us.

STATEMENT OF FAITH ARTICLE *2*

God, who discloses himself to through his creation, has savingly spoken in the words and events of redemptive history. This history is fulfilled in Jesus Christ, the incarnate Word, who is made known to us by the Holy Spirit in sacred Scripture.

SCRIPTURE

In the beginning was the Word,
   and the Word was with God, and the Word was God.
He was in the beginning with God;
   all things were made through him,
   and without him was not anything made that was made.
In him was life, and the life was the light of men.

And the Word became flesh and dwelt among us,
   full of grace and truth;
we have beheld his glory, glory as of the only Son
   from the Father.

                    John 1:1-4,14

CHAPTER *2*

The God Whom We Call Savior

Like a magnet the city of Rome tugged at the attention of the apostle Paul. In his letter to the church there, he shared his frustration at having his trip postponed: "... so I am eager to preach the gospel to you also who in Rome" (Romans 1:15). The details of the voyage that finally fulfilled his ardent wish are chronicled with minute care by Luke in the last two chapters of Acts. It is significant indeed that the history of God's work of salvation in Jesus Christ which Luke wrote in two volumes—his Gospel and Acts—comes to its climax in Rome: "And he (Paul) lived there two whole years at his own expense, and welcomed all who came to him, preaching the kingdom of God and teaching about the Lord Jesus Christ quite openly and unhindered" (Acts 28:30-31).

Paul's concern to bring the gospel to Rome was more than a tribute to the capital of the Empire; it was a tribute to the gospel. The city by the Tiber, to which all roads led, was just the kind of place for which God's good news was designed.

We use words like parochial or provincial to describe ideas that are of interest only to a few people within a limited area. What the east Pasadena little league team does is of interest to a few people besides the parents, the players, and the merchants who serve as sponsors. Their games do not make headlines in Duluth or Birmingham or Lubbock or Moncton. But the Viking landings on Mars and the Voyager photographs of Jupiter do. Though the people who designed and controlled these spacecraft are as much a part of Pasadena as the little league supporters, their work is not provincial. It is as international in importance as it is cosmic in scope. Space exploration is worth noising to the ends of the earth; little league baseball scores are not.

Paul's drive to reach Rome and Luke's delight in reporting his arrival first hand were based on their conviction that the gospel of Jesus Christ's death and resurrection was universal in its impact. Nothing less than Rome was an adequate arena for its proclamation. "The kingdom of God" was the theme of Paul's message; it had imperial significance. Jesus, not Nero, was the true emperor of the universe. God's whole design in history was not the power of the Senate and the Roman people but the revelation of his own grace and glory.

God's relentless commitment to make himself known

The gospel had to clutch the Roman Empire—and any other empire—at its center. It was that kind of gospel. It was the final act in God's program to make himself known, a program whose earliest chapters reached back to creation itself. The unity of God, which we celebrate in our affirmations of the Holy Trinity, insists that the whole creation reckon with him. There is no other God. No members of a divine council can divide the world into spheres of influence, as the League of Nations divided the globe after World War I.

All the creation that there is belongs to the one and only God, Father, Son, and Holy Spirit. And that God has worked insistently to make himself known. The beginnings of that revelatory plan are acknowledged in the Fuller *Statement of Faith* in these words: "God, who discloses himself to through his creation, has savingly spoken in the words and events of redemptive history."

Revelation is what life is all about. Is not that what our evangelical faith affirms? When we list creation and history as the double stage where the divine drama takes place, we are embracing the totality of life. Can we think of any events or experiences that happen to us that are not centered in the world God made and the course of history that he governs?

Relentlessly he is committed to breaking through our ignorance, to piercing our indifference. The whole environment of time and space and things is geared to making God known. His chief agenda item—the demonstration of his holy self—has determined the shape of his creation and the texture of his times.

Revelation sounds a double theme. The stage is double—creation and history—and so is the message of the drama. Psalm 19 catches this as well as any part of Scripture: "The heavens are telling the glory of God; and the firmament proclaims his handiwork" (Psalms 19:1). Glory and majesty are the message shouted by the heavens. Tuned by God to sing his praise, they ceaselessly and boundlessly witness to his power. There is no greater evidence of human blindness and deafness than our failure to discern, the divine canvas, and hear the celestial symphony. Paul had all of us in mind, in our unconverted state, when he spoke of our "ungodliness and wickedness" by which we suppressed his truth: "For what can be known about God is plain to them (to us), because God has shown it to them. Ever since the creation of the world his invisible nature, namely, his eternal power and deity, has been clearly perceived in the things that have been made. So they are without excuse" (Romans 1:19-20).

The second message is necessary because the first has been ignored. "God ... has savingly spoken in the words and events of redemptive history" is the way our Statement summarizes the second theme. "Savingly" is the word to be underscored. Our blindness and deafness to the colors and sounds of creation called for this more penetrating word. It is this emphasis that Psalm 19 includes in its heavenly proclamation: "The law of the Lord is perfect, reviving the soul; the testimony of the Lord is sure, making wise the simple; the precepts of the Lord are right, rejoicing the heart; the commandment of the Lord is pure, enlightening the eyes" (Psalm 19:7-8).

Our deadness, our foolishness, our anxiety, our blindness—with them the instruction of God alone can deal, the instruction given in his word. Through this word comes the story of what God has said and done to save us and of what that salvation means. The guidebook to history, we might call the word. It is the sure account, given by God himself, to help us understand his saving deeds and to respond to them. It is the script—the word is—by which we follow the drama played out on history's stage; and not only follow it but participate in it.

God's relentless commitment to make himself known found him urging Abraham's family from Ur to Haran to Hebron to Egypt. It caused him to pluck up a slave people from bondage and plant them in Canaan. It led him to choose a shepherd as a king, to build a temple in a captured city, to prod prophets to speak on his behalf. That relentless commitment refused to tolerate idolatry because it subverted his purpose and lured his people away from the true knowledge of him; and that commitment sent Paul to Rome to preach the kingdom of God. The dramatic record and the intense consistency of God's commitment are contained in the Scriptures, which are the autobiography of our God who is the Savior.

God's matchless ability to make himself known
No one but God could have penetrated human dullness and crushed human resistance to make himself known. Our evangelical faith pays tribute to this matchless ability. It insists that our knowledge of God is only possible because of who God is. Revelation, not discovery, is the key word in our vocabulary.

That revelation is seen in the wide canvas of creation. When God, like a master artist, stepped back from his easel to look at each stage of his creation, he said, "That is good!" Part of what he meant was that creation was an adequate and accurate display of his own power and deity.

This purpose of creation—or what we call nature—must not be missed. It is more than a display of artistry, though it is an artist's delight. It is no hollow exercise in symmetry, though it is the pattern for the master architects of all ages. Creation is a summons; it is an encounter. It is a gripping, demanding word of God.

In our romantic sentiment we want to see the universe as an expression of inspiring and comforting beauty. Or in our technological age we want to learn from the universe as a masterpiece of engineering. Some, conditioned to think in industrial terms, see the universe as a vast quarry of minerals to be refined and fossil fuels to be consumed.

But God is a purposeful artist, not like a painter I once met at Laguna Beach. Amid the shadowy trees of her canvas I saw mystic white figures—elves, angels, or the like. I asked her what she meant by the painting. With a benign and condescending smile, she answered me; "Whatever you see there is what I meant."

God does not leave the meaning of creation to our interpretation. He used the lavish ability that he alone possesses to make us alert to his existence. He placed us in an environment which not only sustains us but preaches to us of his grandeur and glory.

God has also revealed himself in the long march of biblical history. Talk about ability! Think of using the dull tools and knotty lumber of an ancient kingdom to accomplish purposes of salvation. A slave people and a thirsty land—unlikely ingredients for a transforming revelation; yet God got his will done and made his name known.

No understanding of history will be complete that does not see it as the setting where God spoke the words and wrought the deeds of salvation. History is no mere chronology leading to nowhere. It is not a series of unrelated events nor a meaningless cycle.

History is the place of our salvation. The God who has preached to us through his creation has entered our human politics, economics, and culture to declare by word and work that he is the Savior. He chose and created Israel as his people to broadcast his loving, reconciling grace in our world. History is not just an arena of human activity or a subject for human investigation; it is where the true and living God has manifest his eternal purposes and has held out a saving hand to sinners like us.

Even more powerfully, God has revealed himself in the deep

descent of the Incarnation. The Fuller *Statement of Faith* captures what all evangelicals believe when it declares, "This history is fulfilled in Jesus Christ, the incarnate Word, who is made known to us by the Holy Spirit in sacred Scripture."

Jesus the Christ is the fulfillment of all that God was saying and doing in the course of biblical history. The Christ-event represents the attainment of the goal toward which God had been moving in his plan of salvation for the human family.

God's matchless ability to make himself know was hard at work breaking down the barriers of our resistance. The Word himself had become flesh. The One who had spent eternity in the Father's fellowship now came down to make the Father's glory unmistakably clear.

With increasing precision God had been speaking. His power and diety were revealed in the wonders of nature. His saving concern was demonstrated as he rescued Israel and made them his own. His truth and grace took on our flesh so that we—with mortal fingers—could touch the living God.

Even then human stubborness persisted. History's leading Actor spoke his lines of eloquent love before an unseeing and unhearing audience.

What is the Incarnation? A marvelous display of spiritual information? Yes, and much more. A tantalizing exhibit of miraculous power? Yes, and other things. A compelling curriculum of ethical instruction? Of course, but that is not all. A tragic story which has provided human catharsis so that we can handle further tragedy? No doubt, for some.

But above all, Jesus Christ is the fulfillment, the culmination of God's unbending drive to make himself known as our Savior. In Jesus, the Creator himself walked onto creation's stage to unfold its meaning. In Jesus, history's Lord entered history's limits to bring history to its head. In Jesus, the invisible God made himself flesh to all who would truly see and hear.

And then God took the step to reveal himself in the lasting witness of the Holy Spirit, who brought the Scriptures to their completion. What are the Scriptures—Old and New Testament? The Holy Spirit's testimony to the saving God who came in Jesus. The amazing love and passion of God had shown all along in his government of the minds and pens of human persons. Now the final word had been spoken in Jesus. It became the task of the apostles to give God's own interpretation, his own commentary on that word in the New Testament. Jesus' life, teaching, death, resurrection and ascension were unwrapped by the Holy Spirit as plainly and forcefully as Lazarus, alive from the dead, was unwrapped by his family.

But even the Scriptures—canon completed, sixty-six books in place—did not terminate the relentless commitment to revelation. Wherever the word is read or preached, God the Holy Spirit is yet present to compel us to take it seriously. God continues to prod us along the way that would have us hear and obey.

To Rome Paul was sent. In Rome the kingdom of God was preached. All roads led to and from that great capital. The gospel had to go there. From eternity God had been committed and able to make himself known wherever those roads reached and to all who walked upon them—including us.

STATEMENT OF FAITH ARTICLE 3

Scripture is an essential part and trustworthy record of this divine self-disclosure. All the books of the Old and New Testaments, given by divine inspiration, are the written word of God, the only infallible rule of faith and practice. They are to be interpreted according to their context and purpose and in reverent obedience to the Lord who speaks through them in living power.

SCRIPTURE

But as for you,
    continue in what you have learned
        and have firmly believed,
    knowing from whom you learned it
        and how from childhood
        you have been acquainted with the sacred writings
        which are able to instruct you for salvation
        through faith in Christ Jesus.
All scripture is inspired by God and profitable
   for teaching, for reproof, for correction,
        and for training in righteousness, that the man of God
        may be complete, equipped for every good work.
                II Timothy 3:14-17

CHAPTER *3*

The Scriptures Which We Obey

T here is probably no sound like it in the world. It radiates warmth and tenderness. It conveys compassion and understanding. It confirms a sense of worth and dignity. It may well be the closest earth comes to the music of heaven—the sound of a loving mother speaking gently, almost cooing, to her newborn child.

Condescension without cheapness this speech carries. The mother takes the exquisite joy and the expansive love that she feels and puts them into sounds and syllables. Hers is a task both necessary and impossible. It is impossible because poets and philosophers together would not have the words to describe her love; it is necessary because without comprehension of that love the youngster will grow up stunted and deformed.

So the struggle goes on, hour upon hour, day after day. The rich feelings well up in the depths of the mother's soul, and the soft sounds stammer to express them syllable by syllable. And all the while the baby is beginning to understand. From the stroking fingers on the chafed skin, the baby understands. With ears that need daily swabbing to uncork wax, the baby understands. Through lips that hungrily grasp at a responsive breast, the baby understands.

The mother has moved beyond a preoccupation with her splendid station; she has left aside her seasoned education. She has used all her powers to shrink her vocabulary to infant dimensions. She has compacted gallons of joy and anticipation into tiny drops of communication that she administers as faithfully as she does the morning orange juice. Her baby's total welfare hangs on the reception of that message of love. And the mother tries and tries and tries again. Discouraged by setbacks, she keeps trying. Encouraged by minute signs of perception, she doubles her efforts to get her words across.

Heavenly sounds, we called these. They carry that name because they speak of love. But even more can we call them that because they remind us of the way God has spoken to us. The leaders of the spiritual revival that we call the Reformation—Martin Luther and John Calvin—both spoke of God's language in the Scripture as the baby talk of a mother or a nurse.

Nothing less than good communication was God's aim. The One who had framed us in his image yearned to make himself known to us in all his grace and glory. And he longed, in turn, to hear our words of praise and trust. Think, then, of God's task. His infinite person—matchless in love, holiness, power, righteousness—was to be expressed in terms that our tiny minds and stubborn hearts could grasp.

The drama on a double stage was the method he chose. In the wonders of creation, he declared his might as God of all life; in the events of biblical history, he spoke through Israel's checkered circumstances and especially through Jesus Christ, God in human flesh. With increasing fullness he sought to speak.

At first a mother is content to deal in generalities. She wants her newborn to catch the feeling of her caring. But as time moves on, the expression of that love becomes more specific. The mother shares how she felt when new life first stirred within her and when that life became visible and tangible in her arms. She speaks of things that grieve her love, like carelessness or disobedience. As comprehension grows, communication deepens. The mother's love and the mother's will became ever clearer to the growing child.

The Holy Scriptures, the sixty-six books of our Old and New Testaments, are part of God's activity in making himself abundantly clear. Nothing makes for clarity like words. They are not the only means of expression. Art, music, sculpture, architecture all convey meaning. And body language—the expression on our faces, the gestures of our hands, the way we sit or stand—all have something to say. But for preciseness, for careful communication that has the least possibility of being misunderstood, nothing beats words. God preached his greatness in the heavens and he demonstrated his grace on the cross, but he left neither that preaching nor that demonstration to our interpretation. He gave us words to clinch our understanding as firm and tight as possible. He did this in the Scriptures which we evangelicals seek to obey.

Their revelatory quality
Our Seminary *Statement of Faith* focuses first on the Scriptures as revelation: "Scripture is an essential part and trustworthy record of this divine self-disclosure." As revelation the Bible is different from any other book. That is the first conclusion to be drawn from this statement. Scripture is part of the process of divine disclosure. As essential to God's program for making himself known as any other part, Scripture plays

a key role in what God has been doing since creation. Without it, we would not hear accurately the heavenly sermons thundered at us from the firmament; without it, we would not grasp the love displayed in the Exodus or at Mt. Sinai; without it we could not measure the power to forgive and redeem which was displayed at Calvary and in the empty tomb. Scripture is the scenario drafted by God himself through his prophets and apostles to explain his deeds and words.

Scripture reports what God has done with a trustworthiness which God himself guarantees. But it is more than a record of God's activities, more than a diary of his dealing with Israel and the church. It is itself a deed, an act, an event of revelation. As revelation, the Bible has the power to convey the truth of God as directly as Moses' burning bush, Daniel's handwriting on the wall, or Jesus' calming of the storm. It is a living word of the living God that rings with the power of his loving presence.

Their inspired nature

"Inspiration" is the word we used to describe the unique origin and importance of the Scriptures. While we might refer to other composi-tions of literature, art and music as inspired, inspiration of Scripture is the special activity of the Holy Spirit who produced these writings. The Fuller Statement captures this great evangelical truth in these words: "All the books of the Old and New Testaments, given by divine inspiration, are the written word of God, the only infallible rule of faith and practice."

Inspiration pertains to the whole Bible. God may have chosen diverse persons, differing times and various processes to bring us his word. But he so involved himself in the whole process that all of it—

every book, every paragraph, every line—is his word. Some parts—like the book of Romans—may be more important than others for our understanding of doctrine; some parts—the Psalms or the teachings of Jesus—may speak to us more loudly than other parts when we need strength or comfort; some parts—like the prophecies of Daniel and Revelation—may see the future more clearly than other parts. But none of it, from the genealogies of Genesis to the sacrifices of Leviticus, to the desert wanderings of Numbers, to the politics of Esther, to the lists of friends of the apostle Paul—none of it is not the word of God.

Inspiration makes every part profitable. It was this emphasis that Paul stressed in his instructions to Timothy: "All Scripture is inspired by God and profitable for teaching, for reproof, for correction, and for training in righteousness, that the man of God may be complete, equipped for every good work" (II Timothy 3:16-17).

This reminds us of the mother and the baby. Why all the struggle to communicate? Why all the baby talk and body language? Why all the smiling, cooing, stroking, hugging? The mother's drive is to equip the child to live fruitfully, to give the baby what is needed to cope with life's tests.

God's aim in inspiration is the same. He has not left his people to grow like abandoned weeds on a bleak hillside. He himself has moved holy persons to write the instructions and corrections vital to our personal and spiritual development as men and women of God.

Their infallible character

God's inspiration, with all the mysteries as to how he did it, assures one thing: the Scriptures are precisely what God wanted them to be. His voice rings in every sentence; his thoughts are reflected in every line.

Nowhere else in the whole realm of literature is this true. Churchly documents seek to capture the mind of God, but do so imperfectly. Theologians puzzle over details of Christian doctrine and write their conclusions with faulty pens. Popular leaders make pronouncements about the will of God and are only partly right. Seminary presidents give convocation addresses on doctrinal themes—and pray for forgiveness as they do!

The Bible, evangelicals have gladly affirmed, is the "only infallible rule of faith and practice." The infallible character of the Scriptures means that they will get their message across. History illustrates this. Take the Hebrew prophets, for instance. During their lifetimes they faced rock-like opposition. The powerful and the wealthy were often their adversaries. The common people ignored or disdained their messages. Yet, as they spoke, there were some who believed and preserved their words. And later generations came to feel the truth and power of what they said. Despite the stubbornest kind of opposition the word delivered its message and captured the hearts of God's true people. The same thing happened to the teachings of Jesus. His parables, for instance, confused his friends and enraged his enemies, but did their work nevertheless. They judged unbelievers and instructed believers, as they have continued to do through the centuries.

The basic message, of course, which the infallible word strives to proclaim is the saving mercy of God made possible and made plain in Jesus the Christ. To Timothy, Paul spoke of "the sacred writings which are able to instruct you for salvation through faith in Christ Jesus" (II Timothy 3:15). That powerful ability to lead people to salvation lies at the heart of the Bible's infallibility. Where it is truly preached and lived it will also be believed. The living word will accomplish without fail the purposes of the living God.

The infallible character of the Scriptures also means that they will not deceive us in regard to God's truth. The loving God who has leaned over to speak his saving truths in our childish ears will not lead and has not led us astray. We can count on his teaching to speak the truth when we rightly understand it.

That Holy Scripture is its own interpreter was what Calvin and Luther taught the church. We understand the various parts of the Scripture—profound and puzzling as they are—in light of the whole counsel of God. We test our understanding of more obscure parts in the light of the clearer parts. We check our obligations to obey Old Testament revelation in view of the final words that have come to us through Jesus and his apostles.

Scripture is like a mosaic. All pieces of it are important, fixed there by God himself. Yet only when the pieces are in place can we grasp the whole picture of God's love and grace which is the central theme, the crowning purpose of the Bible. To confuse any combination of the pieces for the truth of the whole is to err from the truth. Scripture is not a collection of infallible rules. Taken as a whole and rightly understood, it is the infallible rule which accomplishes its purpose by leading us to the fullness of God's truth in Jesus Christ.

Their practical use

The Scriptures "are to be interpreted according to their context and purpose and in reverent obedience to the Lord who speaks through them in living powers." These words on the practical use of the Bible deserve more than the passing comment possible here.

Scriptures are to be used in light of their context. Every part of God's word was given in a human situation and written by human hands. Whether the need was a psalm for prayer in sickness, proverbs to help with the raising of children, parables to understand the kingdom of God, epistles to churches struggling with false teachers, or visions of hope to persecuted believers—every part of Scripture was given to meet a specific human need.

Understanding that context and purpose brings us closer to understanding God's word. The human setting of the divine word is not a limitation but a strength. God has deliberately bent over to speak our language and to meet our needs. His word, therefore, is both strange and familiar: strange because it comes from beyond our world; familiar because it was given to flesh and blood within our world.

Scriptures are to be used in view of their power. They are a living and a lordly word. They catch us up in the events they recite. They capture our faith and our obedience.

My mother's stories used to do that. Part of her gift of love to me, as she spoke those heavenly sounds as only mothers can, was to make her past a part of me. I sat by the fire in the farm house in northern New York and heard my grandfather play the flute, though I never saw the man. I laughed as her dog—our dog—followed her to school, sneaking behind the hedges to escape her watchful eye. And I cried when her dog—our dog—died in a losing battle with porcupine quills. Her past became mine, though the events happened thirty years before I was born.

The revelatory, inspired, infallible, useful word of God does that. It snatches us between its covers and tells us what God has been doing. But more than that, because the living Lord yet speaks from between those covers, it makes us know that he is still doing it—still doing it for his church worldwide; still doing it for you and me.

STATEMENT OF FAITH ARTICLE *4*

God, by his word and for his glory, freely created the world of nothing. He made man and woman in his own image, as the crown of creation, that they might have fellowship with him. Tempted by Satan, they rebelled against God. Being estranged from their Maker, yet responsible to him, they became subject to divine   wrath, inwardly depraved and, apart from grace, incapable of returning to God.

SCRIPTURE

These are the generations of the heavens and the earth
* when they were created.*
In the day that the Lord God made the earth and the
heavens, when no plant of the field was yet in the earth
* and no herb of the field had yet sprung up—*
* for the Lord God had not caused it to rain upon the*
* earth, and there was no man to till the ground; but a*
* mist went up from the earth and watered the whole face*
* of the ground—*
then the Lord God formed man of dust from the ground,
* and breathed into his nostrils the breath of life;*
* and man became a living being.*
Now the serpent was more subtle than any other wild
* creature that the Lord God had made.*
He said to the woman, "Did God say, 'You shall not eat of
* any tree of the garden'?"*
And the woman said to the serpent, "We may eat of the fruit
of the trees of the garden; but God said, 'You shall not
* eat of the fruit of the tree which is in the midst of the*
* garden, neither shall you touch it, lest you die.'"*
But the serpent said to the woman, "You will not die. For
* God knows that when you eat of it your eyes will be*
* opened, and you will be like God, knowing good and evil."*

So when the woman saw that the tree was good for food,
    and that it was a delight to the eyes,
    and that the tree was to be desired to make one wise,
    she took of its fruit and ate;
    and she also gave some to her husband, and he ate.
Then the eyes of both were open, and they knew that they
    were naked; and they sewed fig leaves together and
    made themselves aprons.
Then the Lord God said, "Behold, the man has become
    like one of us, knowing good and evil;
    and now, lest he put forth his hand and take also of the
    tree of life, and eat, and live forever"—
therefore the Lord God sent him forth from the garden of
    Eden, to till the ground from which he was taken.
He drove out the man; and at the east of the garden of Eden
    he placed the cherubim, and a flaming sword which
    turned every way, to guard the way to the tree of life.
                      Genesis 2:4-7;3:1-7,22-24

CHAPTER *4*

Humankind to Whom the Faith Is Directed

It happens with tragic frequency. The bride and groom glow with hope as they hurry down the aisle to the stirring stains of Mendelssohn's wedding march. The church is filled with excited well-wishers. Their rosy smiles punctuate oft-repeated remarks like, "Aren't they a lovely couple." "They look so happy." "They seem made for each other." "That's a marriage that can't miss."

Then the blushing exuberance of the wedding plans and honeymoon begins to pale before the dull realities of dishes to be washed, bills to paid, problems to be solved, conflicts to be settled, tensions in taste and talent to be relaxed. The theme of happiness and harmony that sounded through the first movement of the relationship begins to be accented by harsh rhythms and jarring dissonances.

Time wears on and the marriage is further rattled by divergent interests and differences in priorities. One partner seeks a calm, quiet haven in the home; the other wants a varied, frenetic life abuzz with activity. What used to be petty differences become monumental quarrels. And friction dominates the mood.

Finally as the love theme degenerates into frustration, dissatisfaction, and even hostility, the couple give up on their efforts to play the same song. Separation takes place and brings with it the minor chords of loneliness, failure, shame, alienation, and bitterness.

It happens with tragic frequency. Persons who seem made for partnership fall into rebellion and resentment toward the roles that promised them peace and fulfillment.

In a sense the early chapters of the Bible tell that kind of story. They depict a garden wedding—God, the Creator, in rich fellowship with the human pair that he has fashioned from earth's dust and his own breath. Totally the creatures of God, the man and woman are. Even the dust and the rib were his handiworks. With an unsullied oneness God and the couple worked at the tasks of the garden, their magnificent partnership on display to the rest of the creation. What a song they sang together, God and our human parents. Then the notes began to sour—on the human side. Before our very ears the wedding strains give way to the sharp shouts of fleshy rebellion and the sad laments of separation. Three pages in my Bible are all that it takes to shatter that Edenic bliss. Humankind stands on the far side of a rift that seems unspannable even by the constancy of the Creator Lord. Three pages and the character of our human family is indelibly stamped with resentment toward the God who made us and entered into covenant with us.

Our aim here is to trace what happened to our humanity, and where we were left when we broke up the marriage. Evangelicals through the centuries have paid careful attention to the wedding story as Genesis told it because it focuses on human nature and human sin. It is the backdrop against which the gospel comes with its good news. It is important, because it is our story. More than any soul-exposing poem, more than any life-opening drama, more than any heart-rending novel, the first chapters of Genesis disclose the essence of our God-given worth and our human problem. Five great insights about ourselves leap from those priceless pages: 1) we are part of God's creation; 2) we were created for fellowship with him; 3) we have missed his first purpose; 4) we are under divine judgement; 5) we are abandoned to his grace.

Part of God's creation

Like the Apostle's Creed and the Nicene Creed, the Fuller *Statement of Faith* testifies to the work of God the Creator: "God, by his word and for his glory, freely created the world of nothing. He made man and woman in his image, as the crown of creation, that they might have fellowship with him." Our understanding of ourselves begins here. Our basic identity remains confused until we see ourselves as part of God's creation.

We are called to display God's power. We are creatures; we did not just happen as a cosmic accident, a quirk of catalytic chemistry. We are creatures; we can propagate ourselves, but we could not originate ourselves. We are here because of God's power; we have no other adequate explanation.

Our Statement comments on God's power in two ways. First, it repeats the biblical theme that God created "by his word." God's power is so great that creation was no struggle. No enemies opposed his work; no materials put obstacles in his way. He spoke, and it happened. Second, the Statement takes pains to note that God "freely created the world of nothing." An incredible claim this is, and an important one. The powerful God who made us did not need to make us. Further, he needed no help in his creative process. Beyond that he needed no stuff out of which to make his world; no predetermined materials were at hand to limit his work. He used no leftovers from another world; he was not handicapped by the hand-me-downs of deities who had failed.

His magnificent power accounted for all that is. Part of our delight as human beings is to demonstrate and to salute that unique creative power.

We are commissioned to declare God's glory. If God spoke our world into existence with no outside help, then it must be what he wants it to be. He faced no limits that he did not set. Creation is all his work. At each stage he called it good. Why? Because it was perfectly suited to fulfill his purpose. What was that purpose? To make his glory known, to give tangible visible expression to the majesty of his person.

As part of creation, we are designed to participate in that purpose. If the heavens are to declare God's glory—inanimate, impersonal as they are—what then is our human responsibility?

We are not creators; we are not accidents. We were called into being by the power and for the glory of God. We can not understand ourselves until we know this. As persons of God, we are called to declare the glory of God.

Created for fellowship

So far we have fixed our attention on what we human creatures have in common with the rest of creation: made by God's power and for God's glory. But that is only half the story. The other half we have stated like this: "He made man and woman in his own image, as the crown of creation, that they might have fellowship with him."

Comb through the pages of Genesis and you will find that no words like these are used of anything else in the whole creation. The sun and moon are set in their stations to mark the seasons; they were not made for fellowship with God. The plants and fruit trees and vegetation were formed with a capability to reproduce after their kinds; they had no potential for fellowship with God. Only of human beings are these words found: "So God created man in his own image, in the image of God he created him; male and female he created them" (Genesis 1:27).

The best clue as to what is meant by God's image is found in the conversations that follow. As soon as God creates Adam and Eve he begins to talk with them. The garden becomes a forum for conversation. God and humanity converse with each other in a personal way. It is that capability of personal relationship that marks our human kinship with God. He speaks to us, calling himself "I" and calling us "you." And we do the same to him. Physically we are not like God. Size, stature, complexion, facial features—these are terms that do not properly apply to God. Image, then, expresses our personal capabilities. It has to do, first, with the capacity to know and to enjoy another person in the sharing of our innermost thoughts and feelings.

That is why we may speak of God's relationship to us in the language of a marriage. God's greatest gift to us at the beginning was not the order of creation or the beauty of the garden, but the fellowship of his own person and the capability to enter in to that fellowship. We were not made as God's pets but as God's partners.

The language of the Genesis story makes clear that God's image in which we were made also involves the responsibility of personal obedience. Following the creation there come the commands. The human family is called to a fellowship that includes doing God's will.

The grammar turns imperative: "Be fruitful and multiply, and fill the earth and subdue it; and have dominion over the fish of the sea and over the birds of the air and over every living thing that moves upon the earth" (Genesis 1:28). We were told to take charge of the earth and its other creatures. Made in God's image, we were given the abilities and the responsibility to do that. We even had insight clear enough and judgement sound enough to tell the differences between the various animals. As part of our God-given power of speech we had the labels by which to mark these differences, as we named the animals (Genesis 2:20).

But there were limits to our rule. The dominion we exercised had boundaries marked by God: "You may freely eat of every tree of the garden; but of the tree of knowledge of good and evil you shall not eat, for in the day that you eat of it you shall die" (Genesis 2:16-17). Our partnership with God was not a casual alliance; it was a life and death covenant. That tree from which God had barred us was the symbol of the deadly seriousness with which God took our fellowship.

Fallen from his purpose
Fellowship takes many forms. When fellowship works right it takes a form appropriate to the relationship. A married couple may consummate their evening of rich fellowship with sexual intimacy. A church congregation may express their deepest fellowship with an embrace; two business partners, with a handshake.

Fellowship with the president of the United States in the Oval Office takes one form; fellowship with the Cub Scouts in the city park takes another. Each expression of fellowship has its privileges and its limits. Our fellowship with God at the beginning carried the privilege of conversation with him and the responsibility of obedience to him.

What would happen to our fellowship with the president if we tried to brush him aside and sit at his desk? What would be his reaction if we snatched his pen and tried to ink our names on the latest bill that Congress had sent down from the hill? The answer is plain: fellowship would cease. The Fuller Statement speaks of what we did in these terse phrases: "Tempted by Satan, they rebelled against God."

The temptation flowed out of the fellowship. Humanity's first temptation was not to deeds low and lewd. It was not so much a temptation downward as upward. Masking behind a subtle, beautiful serpent—part of the animal world that Adam had given names to—Satan lured the man and the woman to heady heights: " ... you will be like God, knowing good and evil" (Genesis 3:5). Equality with God, with the comprehensive knowledge of all of life in its rights and wrongs—what an upward leap that seemed to be!

But through it we fell. Our prideful, grasping disobedience broke the terms of our fellowship with God. His purpose for us had been the display of his power and glory. With that we were not content. Power and glory of our own were what we craved for and clutched at. Mutiny it was, rebellion. We turned on our garden Friend and tried to snatch the scepter from his hand. And at that moment God's scepter of glory became his gavel of judgement.

Under divine wrath

The elements in this judgement evoke the harshest language in our evangelical faith: "Being estranged from their Maker, yet responsible to him, they became subject to divine wrath, inwardly depraved and, apart from grace, incapable of returning to God."

Alienated from God and disoriented within ourselves—those are the twin facets of judgement. God's dignity could not tolerate the sinful ambition of beings alienated from him and disoriented within themselves.

But the divine wrath that we are under is not only an expression of God's dignity; it is a reflex of his love. Where such vast capability for fellowship exists, the capacity for hurt is enormous. When communication breaks down in that glowing marriage we have been talking about, the intensity of the pain matches the brightness of the glow. The higher the plane of the relationship, the greater the agony of a fall from it. God's wrath that banned us from the garden and set us wandering in search of other homes and other lovers is the direct result of the magnitude of his love—a love that made rebellion utterly intolerable to him.

Something happened in us as well as to us when we grasped at God's power and glory. "Inwardly depraved ... incapable of returning to God" are the phrases used. This does not mean we are entirely bad—as though we could not write brilliant symphonies, build mighty bridges, set up systems of law, write powerful novels, cook tasty meals, discover therapeutic drugs, and speak kind words to neighbors.

It means that our desire to return to God is stone cold. It means that our will to worship him is dead as a door nail. It means that our power to love him and others in the way he intended is completely drained. Whatever else we may be able to accomplish in life, we have no ability on our own to return to God's original purpose. Revealing his power and living for his glory are beyond our human reach. What a deep tragedy! What we were made to do and what we were best at doing are now our sharpest failures. I think of the stainless steel water pots that are designed to soak the teabag into life at the local coffee shop. They have only one duty to perform—to fill the cup, not the tabletop, with water. They fail every time—an outcome we human beings can understand.

Abandoned to grace

That is why I am especially glad for one phrase in this bleak statement about our fallen nature—"apart from grace." Biblical realism takes sin with full seriousness; we must do the same. But the other great reality of the Bible is what we stake our lives on—the reality of God's grace.

Even in the garden at the moment we turned our backs on the marriage, his grace was at work. He called to us in our hiding; he clothed us with animal skins to veil our naked shame. Even the curse of judgement is trimmed with grace: the pain and sweat are there; but so are the hope of childbirth and the possibility of daily bread.

The marriage had been shattered, but from one side only. The grace of restoration and reconciliation would in due season be available. God had promised. For Adam and Eve that was only a dim hope. For us— their sons and daughters, who have felt the promise come to high fulfillment—it is a bright reality.

STATEMENT OF FAITH ARTICLE 5

The only Mediator between God and humankind is Christ Jesus our Lord, God's eternal Son, who, being conceived by the Holy Spirit and born of the Virgin Mary, fully shared and fulfilled our humanity in a life of perfect obedience. By his death in our stead, he revealed the divine love and upheld divine justice, removing our guilt and reconciling us to God. Having redeemed us from sin, the third day he rose bodily from the grave, victorious over death and the powers of darkness. He ascended into heaven where, at God's right hand, he intercedes for all his people and rules as Lord over all.

SCRIPTURE

---

*He is the image of the invisible God, the first-born of all
    creation;*
*for in him all things were created, in heaven and on earth,
    visible and invisible, whether thrones or dominions or
    principalities or authorities—all things were created
    through him and for him.*
*He is before all things, and in him all things hold
    together.*
He is the head of the body, the church;
    he is the beginning, the first-born from the dead,
    that in everything he might be preeminent.
For in him all the fulness of God was pleased to dwell,
    and through him to reconcile to himself all things,
    *whether on earth or in heaven, making peace by the
    blood of his cross.*
And you, who once were estranged and hostile in mind,
    *doing evil deeds, he has now reconciled in his body of
    flesh by his death,*
in order to present you holy and blameless and irreproach-
    able before him, provided that you continue in the faith,
    *stable and steadfast, not shifting from the hope of the
    gospel which you heard, which has been preached to
    every creature under heaven, and of which I, Paul,
    became minister.*   Colossians 1:15-23

First of all, then, I urge that supplications, prayers,
  intercessions, thanksgivings be made for all people,
  for kings and all who are in high positions,
  that we may lead a quiet and peaceable life, godly and
  respectful in every way.
This is good,
  and it is acceptable in the sight of God our Savior,
  who desires all persons to be saved and to come
  to the knowledge of the truth.
For there is one God, and there is one mediator
  between God and humankind,
the man Christ Jesus, who gave himself as a ransom for all,
  the testimony to which was borne at the proper time.
For this I was appointed a preacher and apostle
  (I am telling the truth, I am not lying),
  a teacher of the Gentiles in faith and truth.
                    I Timothy 2:1-7

CHAPTER 5

The Christ Whom we Trust

There is no Mt. Rushmore for the world's great religious leaders. It was a hard enough choice to narrow down the list of presidents to the four massive profiles that jut from that South Dakota mountain peak. Historians and political scientists may debate for decades the merits of the decision that memorialized Washington, Jefferson, Lincoln, and Theodore Roosevelt in granite.

You can image the arguments waging among the admirers of James Monroe, who protected our hemisphere from European intrusion; of Woodrow Wilson, who envisaged an alliance of once hostile powers as a gateway to world peace; of Franklin Roosevelt, whose concern for Americans of lower income sparked sweeping changes in labor and social security legislation; or of Harry Truman, whose blunt courage helped to bring stability in the aftermath of war. Indeed, a whole additional mountain rightly could be dedicated to the achievements of other American presidents.

What is of significance for us is that it took at least a quartet of great men to sum up the power and the vision of the American presidency. No one president would merit a mountain of his own. Not the greatest of them—even were we sure who that might be—could tower over all the others as the unique example of what distinguished leadership should be.

There can be no Mt. Rushmore for the great religious leaders of the centuries. No Gutzon Borglum would devote fourteen years of his life (1927-1941) to the carving of faces seventy feet high for Zoroaster, Buddha, Jesus, and Muhammad. Of presidents, a handful were chosen—men of lavish but virtually equal contribution to the welfare of the land. Of religious teachers, the similarities of credentials are only superficial.

Zoroaster's day has come and gone. His once magnificent following, which numbered in its ranks the proudest kings of Persia, has in our generation dwindled to fewer that 200 thousand scattered from Yezd in Iran to Bombay. It is questionable whether they could muster the resources to pay their share of the sculpture.

Buddha's nearly 400 million adherents would be pleased to contribute to the fund for carving his statue, since images of the Buddha are the chief visible expression of their loyalty. It is doubtful however, whether such grand tribute would have been acceptable to him. His was a simple life, marked by two grand moments: his Great Renunciation, when he turned his back on the wealth and power of his family, and the Great Enlightenment, when the way of salvation from suffering was disclosed to him. He would have viewed himself not as the Light but as the enlightened one, and his human frailty showed itself when he died in Nepal from eating contaminated pork.

Certainly Muhammad's disciples—half a billion strong—could afford to pay their share of a religious Mt. Rushmore, especially if they were allowed to use petro-dollars for their ante. But they would not want to participate in the project at all. For them Muhammad was a seal of the prophets, the last and greatest of the messengers of Allah. No sculpture of him would be allowed for fear of the judgement of Allah who banned all such idols in the law of Musa, as they call Moses. Furthermore, if any part of the Muslim faith were to be preserved in sacred memory, it would have to be the Qur'an for which Muhammad was God's chosen channel.

No sacred Rushmore is possible—not for Zoroaster, nor Buddha, nor Muhammad. And certainly not for Jesus who is called the Christ. His followers viewed him as unique. And so did his Father, who summarily rejected Peter's suggestion that Jesus could share the glory of the mountain with Moses and Elijah. If even the temporary equality of the three huts that Peter proposed was an offense to Jesus, what would he say of others? If the chief law-giver and pioneer of the prophets did not rank with him, how could the only partially enlightened spiritual leaders of the centuries?

No Mt. Rushmore for religious leaders! God himself has banned the project: "This is my Son, my Chosen; listen to him!" (Luke 9:35).

The perfect Mediator

At the heart of our creeds, as at the heart of our faith, stands this Chosen One, this Son. Different from all others, he it is who makes our evangelical belief different from all other systems of religion. Of him the Fuller Statement joyfully confesses: "The only Mediator between God and humankind is Christ Jesus our Lord, God's eternal Son, who, being conceived by the Holy Spirit and born of the Virgin Mary, fully shared and fulfilled our humanity in a life of perfect obedience."

"Incapable of returning to God"—that is the dreary diagnosis of our human condition. The key creature has had a falling out with the Creator. The rift is beyond the creature's ability to repair. The offspring has become an alien with neither the will nor the knowledge to find the Father's house.

Then came Jesus—the perfect Mediator, God's official Go-between, sent by the Father to heal the rift—to become the way home. No one less than God's eternal Son could discharge such responsibility. All the rest of the human family had the disease; only he, could assume the disease and free us from its ravages.

Who else could speak so clearly of the Father's love? Only the Son who had known the fulness of the Father's fellowship could convince an unbelieving people. Who else could reveal so powerfully the Father's righteousness? Only the Son who from the beginning had shared the Father's holiness and majesty could make divine righteousness walk on human legs. Who else could display so tellingly the Father's will? Only the Son who had participated continually in the counsels of the Holy Trinity could by his perfect obedience demonstrate the life in which God delights.

No one less than Mary's little baby could be the perfect Mediator. To be fully human without being faultily human—that was the requirement. No stranger to our humanity could mend a rift as personal as that between God and his children. No angel unhampered by flesh and blood could know our pain or bear our sin. Yet no ordinary member of our race could be our savior. Sinful human physicians bring no healing for themselves. How can they lift the distress of others?

Humanity without sinfulness? Only divine intervention could make that combination possible. Human reproduction only perpetuated the predicament. Something new, something different had to happen for a perfect Mediator to come. It is to that new event in human biography that we testify in the words "being conceived by the Holy Spirit and born of the Virgin Mary." The normal process of human parenthood, operative since Adam had known Eve and she had conceived Cain, was for once suspended. And a sign was given to the whole human family that salvation is God's doing. Its possibility only becomes pregnant at his initiative.

Mary's little baby! The Almighty God come among us to show the love of God for our race! Who else could know the pangs of our humanity without succumbing to its wiles? Mary's little baby! Who else could do the Father's pleasure in a context that had so consistently incurred the Father's wrath?

God's eternal son and Mary's little baby—that is the union that marked the mystery of mediation. The divine Son—living, working, obeying, teaching, healing, dying in the human nature derived from Mary. Fully, truly, part of each party in the great divorce, he is the only Arbiter of a split that would otherwise be permanent.

Jesus the Christ, whose coming the older covenant and the faith of Israel anticipated, is the one perfect Mediator. All that we need in our estranged humanity, the Almighty God has become, so that we might know the divine love for us.

The faithful Reconciler

"By his death in our stead, he revealed the divine love and upheld divine justice, removing our guilt and reconciling us to God." In these words, the Fuller *Statement of Faith* describes the way in which the perfect Mediator becomes the faithful Reconciler.

Not only going between but drawing together is his mission. Nothing less than full faithfulness would accomplish the reconciliation of our alienation from God—a faithfulness that did not shrink from death.

And what a death it was! From its seed sprang forth a field of brilliant flowers in God's good day!

In his death, our faithful Reconciler displayed God's love. "Incapable of returning to God," that was our condition. But did God care? Perhaps his response to our flight from the garden was "Good riddance to bad rubbish!" What reason would he have to keep on loving us? And what evidence did we have that he could love us, when we could scarcely stand ourselves? Jesus' cross settles all the anxiety that stirs such questions. It tells us that our salvation, our journey home, was so central to the Father's love that he spared nothing—not even his Son's life—to make it possible.

In his death, our faithful Reconciler absorbed God's judgement. Love and judgment side by side—that is the mix of which reconciliation comes. That death should have happened to us. We had committed the ultimate crimes: rejection of God, substitution of our works for his person, hostility and aggression toward those whom he made. In comparison with those felonies, the threat on the life of a human ruler is a mild misdemeanor. All of us were on God's most wanted list. We were his archenemies. He had set for us a rendezvous with death.

But in the love of God, Christ kept that appointment in our place. The crimes we had committed were not dismissed; they were dealt with. God's justice was not compromised, but his love was fulfilled.

In his death, our faithful Reconciler defeated the power of sin. "Inwardly depraved and, apart from grace, incapable of returning to God"—that was the human state in which our race for millennia had been bogged down. Slaves to sin we were, enmeshed in wicked social structures and captured by our own selfishness and pride. So perverse was our perspective that we viewed ourselves as free. We were like the schizophrenics in a mental hospital who are profoundly convinced of their own sanity and the madness of everyone else.

We were guilty before God and able only to stew in that guilt or run from it. Then came Jesus, bearing our cross and dying on it. By absorbing sin's punishment, he broke its hold over us. By displaying God's love, he showed us that by grace we count; that our sin—which rendered us worthless and unlovable—has not kept God from conferring worth and love upon us. By upholding God's justice, he demonstrated how passionately God hates our sin and the lengths to which he has gone to break its hold.

Redemption, we call this process. In the faithful Reconciler, God himself has come to buy us out of slavery. Emancipation and freedom are his great gifts. The gates of our prison house have swung open; the chains that bound us have been cut away. God's love and righteousness—not our depravity and alienation—have become the dominant themes of our song, the fresh atmosphere in which we move and breathe.

Jesus the Christ, in total obedience to the Father's plan, has in his own flesh, cleared the way for our return to fellowship with God. He is the faithful Reconciler. All that was needed to accomplish our salvation, he gladly did.

The living Lord

Our statement rolls on to its conclusion with affirmations around which all evangelicals unite: "Having redeemed us from sin, the third day he rose from the grave, victorious over death and the powers of darkness." The faithful Reconciler, the perfect Mediator, has shown himself to be the living Lord.

His sway is universal; he overrides all opposition like a mighty conqueror. Sin, death, darkness were all arrayed against him. Their banners gleamed; their lances glistened; their cavalry pranced. They mounted their final charge that crucifixion morning, and even the sun hid its face from the gore of the battle. When the dusk fell on that bloody day, the enemies counted the casualties and claimed their victory.

But the real outcome came to light with Sunday's dawn. In his very death, the victim had become the Victor. The borrowed tomb became the scene of boundless triumph. Jesus the Christ had borne the brunt of hell's fiercest attack and was now risen again in his body to wield his universal sway. The indefeasible title of conquest was his. His lordship had been given unassailable demonstration.

His claims are exclusive; he sits enthroned as Governor of the world and High Priest of his people: "He ascended into heaven where, at God's right hand, he intercedes for his people and rules as Lord over all." The unique mission is being pushed to its conclusion. The gap between heaven and earth has been bridged. The eternal Son who descended is the risen Lord who ascended. Full fellowship with the Father, full authority over creation, full advocacy for his people, full confidence in the completion of the mission—that is Christ's present station. God's Son, Mary's child, is the one true Lord of all of life. In him, and in him alone, our human nature has found its potential and achieved its true purpose.

Jesus the Christ, in wondrous triumph over all his foes, has taken our humanity, our bone and flesh, to the very side of God. He is the living Lord. All that our victory required, he achieved.

A Mt. Rushmore for religious leaders? Jesus Christ and those who trust him will have none of that. His exclusiveness forbids it: he alone demonstrates God's character; he alone embodies true humanity; he alone rescues from sin; he alone gives new life-eternal life—from the dead.

Besides that, he has already provided his own memorials: a Mediator's table set with bread and wine; a Lord's day that speaks of resurrection; a Reconciler's church that is his very body. Who would be so foolish as to trade any one of these living memorials for the cold, dead granite of a South Dakota mountainside?

STATEMENT OF FAITH ARTICLE 6

The Holy Spirit, through the proclamation of the gospel, renews our hearts, persuading us to repent of our sins and confess Jesus as Lord. By the same Spirit, we are led to trust in divine mercy, whereby we are forgiven all our sins, justified by faith alone through the merit of Christ our Savior, and granted the free gift of eternal life.

SCRIPTURE

"I have yet many things to say to you,
    but you cannot bear them now.
When the Spirit of truth comes,
    he will guide you into all the truth;
for he will not speak on his own authority,
    but whatever he hears he will speak,
and he will declare to you
    the things that are to come.
He will glorify me,
    for he will take what is mine and declare it to you.
All that the Father has is mine;
    therefore I said that he will take what is mine and
        declare it you."
                        John 16:12-15

So then, brethren, we were debtors, not to the flesh,
to live according to the flesh- for if you live according to
the flesh you will die,
but if by the Spirit you put to death the deeds of the body
you will live.
For all who are led by the Spirit of God are sons of God.
For you did not receive the spirit of slavery to fall back in
fear, but you have received the spirit of sonship.
When we cry, "Abba! Father!"
it is the Spirit himself bearing witness with our spirit
that we are children of God, and if children, then heirs,
heirs of God and fellow heirs with Christ,
provided we suffer with him in order that we may also be
glorified with him.

Romans 8:12-17

CHAPTER *6*

The Spirit Who Works in Us

Can we learn a lesson from Bobby Ferguson? He was the elderly man to whom the Iowa State Penitentiary granted freedom a few years ago. For most of his life—fifty-some years—the prison had been his home. Life on the outside proved intolerable. With poignant pleading, Mr. Ferguson asked for permission to return to the familiarity of those walls and cells. The permission was granted. He remained in the only real home he had ever known to the day he died.

Bobby Ferguson's lesson is this: freedom is almost impossible to handle for those who have never known it. Suppose we had been born in prison and for half a lifetime had never ventured outside its walls. Then release comes. The cell door is opened and the guards escort us out. The prison gate swings wide, and we walk timidly outside the walls to face our life's future.

Think how wrong everything would seem. Would food taste right served on porcelain plates, not metal trays? Could we digest our meals without standing in line for them? Would a waiter's dinner jacket look offensive compared with a guard's uniform? And the sleeping arrangements—would organdy curtains seem flimsy security in place of steel bars? Would we toss and turn on the king-size innersprings while nostalgia longed for the hard narrow cot?

The routine of life, would it get to us? Making our choices, setting our schedules, budgeting our time—these would all be experiences for which we had no training. Our freedom, like Bobby Ferguson's, might seem much worse than our captivity.

The unlocking of a cell, the clasping of a pardon, the striding through a gate—these are the context in which freedom may be found. But the full experience of it, the true appropriation of its meaning, is something that cannot be taken for granted.

God knew that. Freedom for his people was his plan. Yet handling that freedom was bound to be a problem for them. That was why God saw to it that the march from the freedom of the Red Sea led to the foot of Mt. Sinai. There God spelled out the terms of freedom: full trust in his plan for their lives, full obedience to his will for their future, full fellowship with him through their worship. A law, a priesthood, a tabernacle were his great gifts to help Israel know and retain the meaning of her new found freedom.

When Jesus came, the extension and the enrichment of that freedom were his aim. Some of his earliest recorded words herald this: "The Spirit of the Lord is upon me, because he has anointed me to preach good news to the poor. He has sent me to proclaim release to the captives and recovering of sight to the blind, to set at liberty those who are oppressed, to proclaim the acceptable year of the Lord" (Luke 4:18-19). As the year of Jubilee meant joy to all of Israel's slaves, signalling their release and return to full status in society, so Jesus' coming meant a jubilee-like joy to our captive, blind, oppressed human family.

Freedom was what he meant to achieve. What is his redemption on the cross but freedom from slavery to sin or law? What is his resurrection from the dead but freedom from the fear of death and hell? What is his ascension to God's right hand but freedom from the ominous spirits that dominate our personal lives and our political systems? What is his intercession with the Father but freedom for the fulfillment of our mission? What is his lordship over history but freedom for a hope-filled future? "So if the Son makes you free, you will be free indeed" (John 8:36).

The guarantor of that free-indeed type of freedom is God the Holy Spirit. His is the task of applying to our lives the benefits of what Jesus has done as perfect Mediator, faithful Reconciler and living Lord. Two aspects of the freedom which the Spirit brings are highlighted in our Fuller Seminary Statement: 1) freedom to believe what is true; 2) freedom to accept what is given.

Freedom to believe what is true

"The Holy Spirit, through the proclamation of the gospel, renews our hearts, persuading us to repent of our sins and confess Jesus as Lord." The heavenly Persuader, come to our world, is one name by which we may call God's Spirit. The objective events of the Christian gospel are part of history. The factual record of Jesus' obedient life, selfless death, bodily resurrection, and heavenly ascension are recorded for posterity by eyewitnesses whose word we have every reason to trust.

We proclaim, therefore, the gospel with the same confidence that the apostles showed when they hurried through the Mediterranean world, turning it upside down. The gospel is God's good news of a love displayed and a judgment absorbed by Jesus Christ. It is a word from beyond, a declaration of divine truth demonstrated in history. It is not a projection of our human longings for love, though it answers those longings. It is not an imagined power to change our lives, though it has power to change them beyond our imagining. The gospel comes to us from without; it is the truth of how God cares, of how we sinners need that care, and of what he has done about that caring.

For us to hear the gospel is one thing; to believe it is another. Here again our human condition works against us. "Inwardly depraved and, apart from grace, incapable of returning to God," we do not believe the truth when we hear it. We have full freedom to cling to spiritual error—that is sin's contribution to us. We have no freedom to believe God's truth; that is, not until the heavenly Persuader speaks to our hearts and wills. He enables us to say "Yes." And we hear within ourselves the "Amen" to what God has proclaimed to all the world.

We must say "Yes" to the truth of our condition as sinners who need Christ's saving work. That is part of repentance. Who can do this without the Spirit's help? We scurry from our failures like rats from a sinking ship. We flip the blame for them back on others—parents, society, government, employers—like soldiers trying to rid the foxhole of a live grenade. We claim that God does not know, or does not care, like juvenile gangs who justify their mayhem by citing police corruption.

But to say, "God, you are right; I have broken your law, worshiped idols, hated my sister ... " is impossible without the Spirit's persuasion. Only he can give that freedom to persons who have spent a lifetime locked up to evading the issue.

We must also say "Yes" to the truth of God's call to turn from that sin. That too is part of repentance. Breaking the patterns of the past is scary. Renouncing an old way of life before we know much about the new is risky. We would rather test the fresh water gingerly before we take the full plunge. There is a terrifying side to freedom for all of us who have practiced so long being prisoners. That is why we need the Holy Spirit to help us cut the tie and move away from our sins to God's new life.

The Spirit of God gives us freedom to say "Yes" to the truth of Christ's lordship over all reality. Turning from sin is one thing; obeying Christ is another. Conversion, by persuasion of the Spirit, involves more than a release from our allegiance to sin; it insists on a declaration of permanent loyalty to Jesus Christ.

The early Christians faced that declaration with both pain and joy. They knew that Jesus' lordly death, resurrection, and ascension had enthroned him as King of the Universe, Emperor of all of history. They heard that word with joy. They also knew that their Roman rulers ascribed that same glory to the Caesars. Who is Lord? Caesar or Jesus? That was life's greatest question, a question they heard with pain. By the hundreds they faced torture and death, joyous in their pain, as they confessed that Jesus is Lord.

Our choice today may not be so dramatic; it is, however, no less decisive. Other lords clamor for our allegiance. Lords of business, labor, education, pleasure, wealth, and lust vie with each other for our obedience. How good of God to send his Spirit to enable us to believe the truth—and confess it—that Jesus is Lord.

Freedom to accept what is given

The Spirit's further work in our lives is expressed in these terms which for centuries have been treasured by evangelicals: "By the same Spirit we are led to trust in divine mercy, whereby we are forgiven all our sins, justified by faith alone through the merit of Christ our Savior, and granted the free gift of eternal life."

We hear those words with the surprised enthusiasm of a poor family that has listened to the reading of a will that left them millions. Gift after gift the reconciling Christ has made possible to those who trust him.

Yet we must not assume that we automatically have freedom to accept those gifts. For one thing we may be so conditioned to our state as slaves and prisoners that we do not believe that release is possible. We may look upon all offers of rescue as the promises of fools that they have no power to fulfill; or as the tricks of knaves whose false promises of salvation are actually displays of meanness.

The freedom to accept what is given can come only as God's Spirit testifies to God's full ability and total sincerity in his offer to lavish his grace upon us.

The freedom to accept what is given is not something that comes naturally to us. We are tempted either to work for what we get or to presume that we deserve it or do not need it. Either way we are in trouble with God. To think that grace can be earned is to downgrade the meaning of grace. To think that grace has already been earned or is not needed is to obscure the horror of our sin.

Only the Spirit of God can free us from such pride and presumptuousness. Only he can prepare us to receive God's favors as gifts—needed but unearned and unmerited.

Who could earn the gift of divine mercy? Mercy earned would not be mercy at all. Mercy at its heart suggests kindness and compassion to the helpless. Its best analogies are the father's attitude to a tiny child in distress, a nurse's attention to a paralyzed patient, the response of caring to the homeless victims of a hurricane. Multiply these examples by infinity and we have something like God's willingness to stoop to our weakness.

But the analogy breaks down at one point: babies, invalids, disaster victims know their helplessness and admit it. They welcome mercy. Sinners by nature do not. We assume that we do not need it, or that we are beyond its reach, or that there are too many strings attached. The real proof of God's mercy is that he sends his Spirit to help us stubborn ones receive his mercy.

Who could merit the gift of forgiveness and justification? The very language suggests that all merit is ruled out. Sin, not merit, is the subject. What we had earned was judgement. What we have received is forgiveness. That is the surprising way that grace works.

It is grace so surprising that we need freedom to receive it. To forgive is not an easy virtue to cultivate. Blaming ourselves or others for the wrongs done comes much more naturally. Believing that God has truly set our sins behind him and has cleared the way for us to be in good standing with him is not the same as believing that a ship will float or a plane will fly. Our innermost bent fights against the idea that the Lord of all has really said "Yes" to us. And trying hard to believe does not help a lot. Saving faith is not something at which we work, like learning to spell or swim. It is the gift of God's Spirit who drowns our doubts, quells our suspicions, and opens our hearts to receive the gifts that Jesus Christ has made possible.

Nothing less than full freedom was God's plan for the prisoners that Christ's redemption has released. He did not intend us to follow Bobby Ferguson's fateful steps back to prison. The Spirit's full freedom makes us more than spectators watching the events of salvation history unfold at the manger, the cross, the tomb, the mount of ascension, the right hand of the Father. Full freedom—God's freedom—is the freedom to participate in that history, to have our names written into the story as we believe its truth and accept its gift. How great of Father and Son together to send the Holy Spirit to work that freedom in us—and to keep us free!

STATEMENT OF FAITH ARTICLE 7

God graciously adopts us into his family and enables us to call him Father. As we are led by the Spirit, we grow in the knowledge of the Lord, freely keeping his commandments and endeavoring so to live in the world that all may see our good works and glorify our Father who is in heaven.

SCRIPTURE

"You are the salt of the earth;

but if salt has lost its taste, how shall its saltness be
restored?

It is no longer good for anything except to be thrown out and
trodden under foot by humankind.

You are the light of the world.

A city set on a hill cannot be hid.

Nor do men light a lamp and put it under a bushel,

but on a stand, and it gives light to all in the house.

Let your light so shine before all people,

that they may see your good works and give glory to your
Father who is in heaven."

Matthew 5:13-16

I mean that the heir, as long as he is a child,
> *is no better than a slave, though he is the owner of all*
>> *the estate;*

but he is under guardians and trustees until the date set by
> *the father.*

So with us; when we were children, we were slaves to the
> *elemental spirits of the universe.*

But when the time had fully come, God sent forth his Son,
> *born of woman, born under the law, to redeem those who*
>> *were under the law, so that we might receive adop-*
>> *tion as sons.*

And because you are sons, God has sent the Spirit of his Son
> *into our hearts, crying, "Abba! Father!"*

So through God you are no longer a slave but a son,
> *and if a son then an heir.*

Galations 4:1-7

CHAPTER 7

The Life Which We Are Called to Live

None of them will do it. None of the standard illustrations of before-and-after change is strong enough to catch the picture. Neither the dieter who loses 150 pounds, nor the wallflower who is transformed into the life of the party. No change within human capability is radical enough, bright enough, drastic enough to depict the transforming power of God's grace in Jesus Christ.

The Fuller *Statement of Faith* (Article IV) captures the dynamics of this change. Here are the stark lines in the portrait of our before: "... rebelled against God, ... estranged from his Maker, ... subject to divine wrath, ... inwardly depraved, ... incapable of returning to God." Then, in Article VII, we are re-introduced to a whole new aspect of Christian experience: "God graciously adopts us into his family and enables us to call him Father." The intervening sentences have made all the difference: Jesus the Christ—perfect Mediator, the faithful Reconciler, the living Lord—has blazed the way home. The Holy Spirit—the heavenly

Persuader, the Giver of Faith-has turned our steps to follow that way, enabling us to believe God's truth and receive God's gift. Two paragraphs our Statement takes to tell the story; twenty-three lines to chronicle history's most dramatic transformation.

If the alienation was tragic, the reconciliation is triumphant. If the depravity was total, rendering us incapable of coming to terms with God, the renewal is all-embracing, reshaping all our attitudes and activities. None of the usual contrasts of before-and-after is bright enough to illuminate this transformation.

For it, the Bible reserved its strongest metaphors. What is it like to be changed by the love of the Father, the grace of the Son, and the power of the Spirit? Is it like the delight of moving from the slums to the penthouse? Yes, but much more, because money cannot buy it: it is a complete change of citizenship—a move from the kingdom of darkness to the kingdom of light. Is it like the relief of finding that what we thought was a grave disease will respond to medical treatment? Perhaps, but that goes not nearly far enough: it is the ultimate difference in vitality—a resurrection from death to life. Is it like the new lease on life that comes from conquering addiction to alcohol or heroin? Yes, but this too falls short: it is like a new birth–a completely new person starting afresh at the business of living.

Two aspects of this total transformation are spotlighted in our Fuller Statement: God's people have been changed 1) from slaves to children; and 2) from rebels to witnesses.

From slaves to children

One thing we have tried not to leave in doubt: that the entire transformation is an act of God. Listen to the way in which his initiative dominates the sentence: "God graciously adopts us into his family and enables us to call him Father." His adoption is an act of his grace; our freedom to call him Father comes from his enablement. His voice that created the world and his hand that shaped its history are still working to link our lives to his.

The dramatic figure of speech that our Statement seizes is adoption—the change of state from slaves to children. This needs a bit of explaining, because in our society adoption takes a somewhat different form. Our day is different than the first century because orphans or children born out of wedlock are those we adopt. In the world of Jesus and the apostles, heads of households—especially if they were childless—sometimes adopted their slaves and gave them the full rights of sonship. It was an act of grace which totally changed the status and the privileges of the person adopted.

Again, our society has a hard time grasping what adoption meant to the adopted one, because the supply of healthy children to be adopted is so limited that prospective parents sometimes wait years for the opportunity to adopt a youngster. The element of grace, then, that looms large in God's adoption of us, is often obscured. We count it a privilege to be able to adopt a child; the ancient world placed the privilege on the other side. Paul reminded the Galatians of this privilege: "So with us; when we were children, we were slaves to the elemental spirits of the universe. But when the time had fully come, God sent forth his Son, born of woman, born under the law, to redeem those who were under the law, so that we might receive adoption as sons" (Galatians 4:3-5).

Even more brightly does God's grace shine in this passage. We were not even God's slaves when he adopted us. We were slaves to the superstitions of religious ignorance that worshiped the elements and feared the stars. Yet God took us into his family.

Christ's people are adopted children who enjoy the full rights of sonship. Sonship in Scripture is not a right that applies to males alone, although it is a masculine term drawn from a society that accorded its sons higher privileges in authority and inheritance than did its daughters. But the apostle Paul had just dictated his sweeping affirmation which leveled all spiritual differences of race, status, or sex: "There is neither Jew nor Greek, there is neither slave nor free, there is neither male nor female; for you are all one in Christ Jesus" (Galations 3:28). Sonship, therefore, is for all of us-male and female; it is a spiritual privilege, granted by God's grace, not an accident of gender.

The rights of our sonship include full fellowship with the Father. Paul noted this with joy: "And because you are sons, God has sent the Spirit of his Son into our hearts crying, 'Abba! Father!'" (Galations 4:6). Think of the change that the psyche of a slave would have to undergo to call the master by any more intimate term. All the years in which he had been conditioned to bow and call him "Lord" or "Sir" would have to be undone. And all the profanity with which he had secretly addressed his owner in moments of wrath had to be erased. You can almost hear the lump in his throat, the catch in his vocal cords, when he first responds to the master's command to call him "Father."

Are we any different? Our names for God before we have come to know him in Jesus may well have been uttered in moods that range from apathy to disdain to terror to blasphemy. It is a measure of how well God knows our weaknesses that he has sent his Spirit to help us learn the family name and to call him Father—or even more intimately, "Daddy," as the Aramaic word "Abba" suggests. It is the sit-down-and-tell-me-your-troubles, the crawl-on-my-knees-and show-me-where-you-hurt name. Nothing less than that kind of full fellowship with the living God is what it invites.

Christ's people are equipped children, whom the Spirit is preparing for loving service. A clause from the Fuller Statement puts it like this: "As we are led by the Spirit, we grow in the knowledge of the Lord. ... " The transformation from slaves to children is a radiant one. Remember what led us in our slave days: superstitions, as we feared the spirits of the universe; astrology, as we were cowed by the movements of the constellations; legalism, as we bowed to the requirements of the pagan or Jewish religious systems. Now we have a better Leader. The Holy Spirit nudges and prompts, cajoles and woos, with one aim in mind: to help us know the Lord more clearly and more intimately. He who teaches us to call God "Father" and Jesus "Lord" stays by us and in us to help us plumb the depths of that fatherhood and that lordship.

This growth in spiritual knowledge is both a means to further service and an end in itself. Put briefly and simply, we are growing more like Christ as the Spirit teaches us of him: "And we all, with unveiled face, beholding the glory of the Lord, are being changed into his likeness from one degree of glory to another; for this comes from the Lord who is the Spirit" (II Corinthians 3:18).

Christ's people are obligated children, whose voluntary desire to serve surpasses anything they had known in their slave days: "Freely keeping his commandments" is the way our Statement describes this new life. As part of the family, we now have a stake in the enterprise: "So through God you are no longer a slave but a son, and if a son then an heir" (Galatians 4:7). Intimate fellowship and ultimate inheritance are the twin gifts of sonship. And with them comes the higher obligation to do the Father's will.

Like children in a family business, we give ourselves to the work with willing heart and eager hand. To New York came the Circus Vargas—a regular circus with trucks and tents and roustabouts. The editor of a national magazine wrote of taking an old friend, a circus buff, to see the show. Afterwards they were delighted to meet Cliff Vargas, the owner of the circus. "You were the man who took our tickets!" the amazed old man exclaimed. "That's right," Vargas relied, "we're all one family. We all do what we have to do."

If a circus works that way, how much more the family of God? We all do what we have to do—in loving God and serving others. The change of status from slaves to children makes us free to lose ourselves in that kind of work. Jesus, the elder brother, is himself both Son and Servant. His sense of obligation to the Father's will and work sets the pace for ours.

From rebels to witnesses

God's before-and-after has worked its magnificent changes. He has taken a crowd of slaves—serving religious regulations, primitive fears, inordinate lusts—and made us a family, calling him Father, growing to know him, keeping his commandments. The change could be put another way: God has turned rebels into witnesses. We who had been dead-set against him now testify to his glory: "endeavoring so to live in the world that all may see our good works and glorify our Father who is in heaven."

The life to which we are called by God's Spirit is a life that does good works. The context in which Jesus spoke of this life makes clear what such works entail: devotion to the person of God, love for the unlovely, passion for justice, inward and outward righteousness, regard for peace, joy in persecution and a call for others to join us in converting to God.

What a wondrous way to live! These deeds, prompted by God's Spirit and demonstrated by Jesus himself, are rightly called "good"-and for many reasons: they give pleasure in the doing; they provide satisfaction in their results; they lead us to share in God's own mission in the world. They are good deeds because they are the kinds of things God himself does. They are the Father's way being followed by his Spirit-led children.

The life to which we are called by God's Spirit is a life that glorifies the Father. It is a life which smacks of revelation; we become the epistles in which others can read about God in their own languages. What glorifies God more than for others to recognize and revere his glory? What is a higher human purpose than for us to live in such a way that men and women will say, "Ah, now I see; that is what God is like!"

In the sixties, children from all kinds of families fled their homes to find a new way to live their lives. Suffocating in the emptiness of their time, they sought to breathe a transcendent air where meaning and real purpose could soothe their longings. They often found but desolation and death. The sea-changes they endured were not the transformations they needed. Our culture struggles still to understand their cries. But obviously, the change for which they hoped has not yet come to our civilization. The question is still asked: "The Great Society—did it come and go, is it yet to come, was it just talk, or what?"

May not this remind us of what Christ has meant for millions of people throughout the centuries—God's great society bringing the quality of his own life into the kitchens and shops, factories and offices, schoolrooms and laboratories of our broken society. The before of our fallen world has ample demonstration on every corner. Slaves and rebels we meet on every hand. Can we pray God to help us more than match them with dramatic and consistent examples of his after—the remarkable changes which his grace has worked in turning rebellious slaves into witnessing children? May the God of all glory get glory for his name as he gives us grace to call him Father and do that Father's will.

STATEMENT OF FAITH ARTICLE **8**

God by his word and Spirit creates the one holy catholic and apostolic Church, calling sinners out of the whole human race into the fellowship of Christ's body. By the same word and Spirit, he guides and preserves for eternity that new, redeemed humanity, which, being formed in every culture, is spiritually one with the people of God in all ages.

SCRIPTURE

For just as the body is one and has many members,
  and all the members of the body,
    though many, are one body, so it is with Christ.
For by one Spirit we were all baptized into one body—
  Jews or Greeks, slaves or free—and all were made to
    drink of one Spirit.
For the body does not consist of one member but of many.
                    I Corinthians 12:12-14

CHAPTER *8*

The Church to Which We Belong

Archeology is one way of getting at human history. With shovels and trowels we dig around ancient sites and try to clean away the rubble so that the ruins of a civilization will tell us something of their story.

The design of the buildings and the materials with which they were constructed tell us about the art and technology of the early inhabitants. As important as any other clues are the tools, weapons, and pots used by the occupants at each stage of their history. Were their knives and axes made of stone, bronze, or iron? The answer to that question tells us much about the degree of development that their civilization enjoyed. Was their clay pottery turned on a wheel or handmade? Was it baked in a kiln or sun-dried? Was it highly decorated or plainly crafted? The answer to these queries convey to the practiced mind worlds of information about the life and culture and time of the long-gone men and women who used those pots.

Archaeologists have an eye out for strata—the various levels of civilization which pile one upon another as one set of buildings crumble and are built upon by a later generation. Their shafts are like journeys through the various stages of the past. The deeper the shaft penetrates the silt and the rubble of an ancient mound the further back into history the archaeologists peer.

And at each stage, the questions are put: Who were these people? What were they doing? What were their lives like? How did they do their work? And from architecture, tools, pottery, art, and especially written documents—like clay tablets, papyrus scrolls or inscriptions on walls—we have been able to understand the values, the purposes, and the missions of dozens of ancient civilizations.

If we applied a similar technique to biblical history, what would we find out about God's activity in history? How would we describe what he was doing stratum by stratum?

At the deepest levels of the shaft, he was setting the stage for his program to make himself known by creating a man and woman in his likeness—a man and a woman who were commissioned to begin the process that would fill the earth with persons who were capable of loving and serving God. Moving up the shaft, we come to Abraham's stratum and discover that God has called one family into a special relationship with him. Then up to Moses' level, where we find that God has rescued a host of Abraham's descendants from slavery in Egypt and has constituted them a nation whose clearest distinctive was to be their loyalty to him.

Up and up we could climb, examining the results of God's activity at each level: he established a kingdom under David to give a political structure to his program; he destroyed that kingdom in Jeremiah's day to show that disloyalty to him is history's greatest crime; he rebuilt

Jerusalem and its temple through Zerubbabel and Nehemiah to demonstrate the persistence of his love; he visited our planet in Jesus Christ to show us his fullness and draw us to himself by the power of the cross.

What God has been doing he has left ample record of in the course of history and in the Scriptures, which are like a handbook of spiritual archeology. As we climb toward the top of the shaft, we might well ask, "What is God doing now? How is his purpose carried out in the stratum of which we are a part?"

His own answer, readily discerned in the Bible and in the two thousand years of Christian history, would be something like this: "I am at work in the world through the Church—the people whom I have called to trust, love, and serve me."

The work of revelation begun at creation came to its fruition in the life, words, and acts of Jesus the Christ. All that we need to know about divine truth and human life is revealed in him. All that it took to reconcile us to God was accomplished by him. Enemies that narrowed and choked our existence—the devil, the world, the flesh—were all conquered by him. Sin, death, and hell itself were trampled in that conquest.

Now God's mission is to spread the news of that victory to every tribe, people and nation. To do this he has chosen a new people, a new Israel, the church. The church in one sense is God's means of heralding and demonstrating his saving purpose to the world. In another sense, the church is one of God's ends, one of his goals in history—the forming of a people to praise him and to live in the love of Him.

The creation of the church
The Fuller Statement keeps the spotlight on God even as it describes the

Christian church: "God by his word and Spirit creates the one holy catholic and apostolic church, calling sinners out of the whole human race into the fellowship of Christ's Body."

The church is created by God's own activity. Created is the right word. When God chose the church as a channel through which his love would flow to the world, he did not select any organization then existing. Not the Roman third legion, nor the Jewish Sanhedrin, nor the Egyptian palace guard did he choose. He did not arbitrarily reach down and elevate one social or national group over another. Even the twelve apostles were gathered only one or two at a time. He fashioned something new to discharge his purpose, as he had founded a new people from Abraham's loins.

Only divine activity could form such a people. There were no other binding ties but the compelling word and the convincing Spirit. Everything else about the church would have divided it from the beginning. It was ripe for great social conflict between slaves like Onesimus and masters like Philemon. It was prone to racial struggle between Jews like Peter and Gentiles like Cornelius. It was exposed to cultural stress between Palestinians like Barnabas and Egyptians like Apollos.

Within a few decades of the resurrection it had overleaped boundaries and united people from the banks of the Euphrates to the cataracts of Egypt, from the Cicilian Gates near Tarsus to the Praetorian barracks at Rome. Only through the word with its news of God's powerful love and only by the Spirit with his ability to make that news personal could Christ build such a church. Centuries have made it only more diverse as they have amplified its testimony to its divine origins.

The church is stamped with God's own character. It is one, because he is one. He has only one mission, only one unified purpose, only one redemptive program, only one human family, and only one society to minister to that family—the one church of the living God "built on the foundation of the apostles and prophets, Christ Jesus himself being the cornerstone, ..." (Ephesians 2:20).

The church is holy, because God is holy. Our holiness as a Christian fellowship is not a quality which we have achieved or attained. It is a holiness given to us by virtue of our relationship to the holy God. The holy word, preached to us in the gospel, has called us into being, and the Holy Spirit has come to dwell within us. This call and this indwelling set us apart from the world with a holiness derived from God's own person.

The church is catholic, because God made and loves the whole world. His concerns for human salvation and his commitments to human welfare are universal. There are no nooks and crannies of our globe where he does not want his glories to shine and his name to be adored. Because the world is God's mission field, it is also ours. There are no places where God's church is not at home, no races who cannot be called to join it, no cultures where it will not thrive.

The church is apostolic, because it shares in God's own mission. It is sent into the world to continue the commission which Christ himself obeyed and which his special messengers, the apostles, carried out to the margins of the Greco-Roman world. In Jesus, God himself became a missionary—an apostle, if you will—dispatched with an indispensable mission and an irreplaceable message. There can be no true church which is not apostolic, for there is no other divine mission and no further divine message.

This church, stamped with God's own character—one holy catholic and apostolic church—lives in fellowship with Christ as his body. Taking their direction from him who is their head, all the members put their Spirit-given gifts to the task of extending his mission throughout the world for which he died.

The preservation of the church

The Fuller Statement goes on to describe God's care for that church to which all Christian believers belong: "By the same word and spirit, he guides and preserves for eternity that new, redeemed humanity, which, being formed in every culture, is spiritually one with the people of God in all ages."

God's guidance and preservation go hand in hand. The one leads to the other: God preserves the church by guiding it through his word and Spirit. Preservation without such continued guidance might prove stultifying.

The means of God's preservation is his renewal. Throughout history he has worked this way. He kept his earlier people Israel going by fresh deeds of grace and judgement; he does the same for his later people. By the conversion of unbelievers from the world, he refreshes his church. As the word and Spirit lead outsiders to faith and repentance, insiders find their faith strengthened and their allegiance tightened. And as the outsiders become insiders the church's witness to other outsiders is enhanced. By the renewed obedience of the church to the world's demands and Spirit's urgings, the church is preserved. The revivals on every continent during the past century or so are part of God's gifts of preservation and guidance. And so are fresh dedication to mission across cultures and to the cause of justice at home.

The scope of God's preservation reaches to every culture and to all eternity. What else would we expect of the Creator-Redeemer-Lord? No culture is foreign to him; none represents insuperable obstacles to his word and Spirit; none is so avid that the church cannot be planted in it, watered, and tended; all are part of the stratum in which God is at work in our age. Surface archeology, which ranges over the tops of history's mound, can testify that almost anywhere on the globe where populated areas are found, a Christian fellowship can be reached within one day's journey on foot. The church is alive and well-guided and preserved by the vital word, invigorated and refreshed by the winds of the Spirit.

Nothing that time or history will bring can change this. Here our archaeological analogy breaks down. Archeology basically presses from present into past, meter by meter, level by level. As it reads that stretching shaft to yesterday and the day before, it makes its comments on today. It puts our present in the context of what led up to it. But there it stops. It has no tools for digging into tomorrow.

What archeology cannot reach, biblical faith can joyfully affirm. Archeology strives to read the records of the past. But biblical faith knows the Builder, who stage by stage has made his promises and kept them.

On the knowledge of his character and the pledges of his word, we look into the future and see there a triumphant church. The program of God will be consummated with glory; the people of God will be blessed with the Father's eternal fellowship. What God has begun and continued, he will see through to a climax marked by his own splendor.

The church, glorious in its creation and magnificent in its preservation, has no room for complacency. The knowledge that God has brought it into being and the hope that he will see it through to triumph must only be incentives to more faithful service.

What we the church are by divine blessings of unity, sanctify, universality and mission, we must seek to display in our earthly service.

The prayer of the church from the beginning has been: "Thy will be done, on earth as it is in heaven." By God's grace we are enabled not only to voice that petition but to be part of its answer.

STATEMENT OF FAITH ARTICLE **9**

The Church is summoned by Christ to offer acceptable worship to God and to serve him by preaching the gospel and making disciples of all nations, by tending the flock through the ministry of the Word and sacraments and through daily pastoral care, by striving for social justice and by relieving human distress and need.

SCRIPTURE

For the grace of God has appeared for the salvation of all men,
    training us to renounce irreligion and worldly passions,
        and to live sober, upright, and godly lives in this world,
        awaiting our blessed hope, the appearing of the glory of
        our great God and Savior Jesus Christ,
who gave himself for us to redeem us from all iniquity
    and to purify for himself a people of his own
    who are zealous for good deeds.
Declare these things; exhort and reprove with all authority.
Let no one disregard you.

Titus 2:11-15

"Go therefore and make disciples of all nations,
　　baptizing them in the name of the Father and of the Son
　　　　and of the Holy Spirit,
teaching them to observe all that I have commanded you;
and lo, I am with you always, to the close of the age."
　　　　　　　　　　　　　　Matthew 28:19-20

CHAPTER *9*

The Church in Which We Serve

I have watched it change from stage to stage. It is an old house at the corner of Hudson and California, just a few blocks from our apartment in Pasadena. Like hundreds of other homes in that area, it had an elegance so faded as to be hardly recognizable. Layers of peeled paint encrusted the outside like barnacles on the hull of a derelict ship. The fluted columns that held the portico in place showed the decades of benign neglect. Screens were tattered; windows were cobwebbed; iron railings rattled in the wind.

Then things began to change. They were hardly perceptible at first. Sprawling bushes that shrouded the porch were stripped away. Layers of paint that armored the pillars were scraped into piles of rubble. One by one the details of the facade that had produced such pride in the first owners were given the attention for which they were starved. Rich redwood began to appear from under pallid paint. Leaded windows again primly framed panes of glass made whole.

Week after week I watched the progress of the crews in their ministry of restoration. I came to share their delight as the splendor of the noble edifice began to shine again. Crumpled stucco was patched, sealed, primed and painted. Wrought iron railings were restored to their original gleaming luster. Bright yellow shutters were hung at the windows. The house now presents an image of newness and beauty it had lost for a lifetime.

Such restoration may interest us for more reasons than aesthetic delight or civic pride. In a sense, restoration is what history is about. Restoration is what our world needs; restoration is what God is doing. Can this be the reason that we find the restoration of old and used things such a satisfaction? Is it possible that when we restore order out of ancient chaos—refurbishing houses, refinishing furniture, repairing china, repolishing brass or silver—we are writing parables about ourselves? In such projects do we vicariously experience that restoration our damaged humanity longs for? Unwittingly, as we restore the old to the new, are we seeking to cooperate in God's great venture?

What is the Bible about but the story of what we did to ourselves and God's whole creation to corrode the primary purposes of the Father God? What is the Bible about but his consistent efforts to bring renewal to a world and a family aged before its time? And what is the Bible about but the story of the church as the society in whom and through whom God is bringing about the cosmic restoration?

It is nothing less than this restoration—this recreation, if you will—that is the church's mission as expressed in our Fuller *Statement of Faith*: "The church is summoned by Christ to offer acceptable worship to God and to serve him by preaching the gospel and making disciples of all nations, by tending the flock through the ministry of the Word and sacraments and through daily pastoral care, by striving for social justice and by relieving human distress and need." Worship which does God's will and service which fulfills God's program—these are kindred cords which are braided together where the church perceives and fulfills her part in God's mission.

Worship which does God's will

"Acceptable worship" is brief, almost shorthand phrase with which the Statement describes the first strand. Its full colors and texture are on lavish display throughout the pages of the Scripture. Through the merits of Christ and in the power of the Spirit, we approach the triune God in wonder, love, and praise.

Acceptable worship begins with adoration of God's name. How can restoration be accomplished without that? Our failure here was what caused our collapse in the first place. We were not content to bear our own names as "man" and "woman," and we were not content to give names to the animals as a badge of our ability to regulate their conduct and understand their nature. We wanted to share God's name. "You will be like God" (Genesis 3:5) was an offer we found too enticing to turn down. We preferred to lay claim to his name rather than to bow down before it. At the Tower of Babel, our forebears reinforced our sinful ambition: "Come, let us build ourselves a city, and a tower with its top in the heavens, and let us make a name for ourselves ... " (Genesis 11:14). The grasping after a name that carried weight in heaven—that is the heart of our human error.

Only when ambition for God's name is replaced by adoration of it does restoration begin. The church enters into God's cosmic plan for renewal as it receives grace to adore God's name, to honor him as true and living Lord.

Acceptable worship continues with appreciation of God's gifts. We do not create anything. Every ounce of our existence is derived. "Naked I came from my mothers womb, and naked shall I return" (Job 1:21) was the way Job described our human lot. Everything we get along the way is a gift, and so, of course, is that naked hank of bone and hair with which our life begins.

Again, we went wrong from the beginning. What was it that pushed us to grasp for fruit forbidden if it was not ingratitude for fruit permitted? What was it that lured us to climb for higher status if it was not ingratitude for our role as lordly servants?

How much that has damaged our world and lives is the corruption spawned by that first ingratitude! Envy, lust, stealing, selfishness all suggest that we think our lot ought to be better than it is. Because we are not grateful for God's grace we demean ourselves, exploit his creation, question his plans, and blaspheme his name.

Restoration must include the worship that views life's crowning reality as the worth of God. When it does, gratitude for how he works and what he gives will follow.

Acceptable worship includes obedience to God's commands. How else do we know that worship is worship of God? Worship is not a peculiarly Christian experience. Humankind is the worshiping animal. Adoration, gratitude and obedience are things that we are made for and good at. Our problem is not aptitude but misdirection. We adore the wrong names, thank the wrong parties, obey the wrong commands.

To obey God's commands, then, is essential to worship that is acceptable. Worship so values God's worth that it regards it as the norm for all of life. God's standards must become ours or worship is sacrilege. That is what commands are for, to help us be like God in righteousness and love. We turned our backs on his lordship at the beginning and consigned ourselves to chaos as we did. The old house has no possibility of being made new unless obedience is a central component of the reconstruction.

What is Christ's church? It is the community of restoration, the company which the triune God is reviving and through whom life is offered to the world. What are we as Christ's church? We are the crowd called to sing the right songs. We are the "Glory be to the Father and to the Son and to the Holy Ghost" congregation who adore God's name and worship him for who he is. What are we as Christ's church? We are the "praise God from whom all blessings flow" people, grateful to God for what God gives. What are we? We are the free to "trust and obey for there's no other way" society, who honor God by doing what God commands. We are a circle of love that celebrates the freedom of obedience in words like these:

"There's a wideness in God's mercy,
Like the wideness of the sea;
There's a kindness in His justice,
Which is more than liberty."

Service which fulfills God's program

Tied to the church's worshipful obedience is the other cord of diligent service. Restoration is not magic; it is mission. And that means hard work. The power of the new creation, like all power to create, is God's alone. But in his grace he has not usually chosen to use that power apart from the efforts of his special people, who are enabled to enter into Christ's service empowered by the Spirit.

Evangelization plays an indispensable part in those efforts. No evangelical creed can be all that it wants to be without this crucial emphasis. Our Statement notes that Christ's church is summoned by our Lord "to serve him by preaching the gospel and making disciples of all nations."

Biblical evangelism involves a message, a purpose, and a context. The message is the gospel—the good news that Jesus has come to reveal God's love and to save us from his wrath. Christ's death and resurrection are the twin pillars on which the good news rests: "For I delivered to you as of first importance what I also received, that Christ died for our sins in accordance with the scriptures, that he was buried, that he was raised on the third day in accordance with scriptures, ..." (I Corinthians 15:3-5). Jesus' death and resurrection have defeated the enemies, sin and death, that defended the old status quo. And restoration is now possible, now underway. That is the welcome announcement.

The purpose of evangelization is discipleship. The church's task is not to bomb villages with leaflets proclaiming good news. It is to tell and live that good news in such a way as to encourage decision for Christ and to ground in the fellowship of Christ's people those who decide.

The context of evangelization is the world. What else? That is the arena which God made. It is the setting with which the biblical story begins and ends. The whole place—every person, people, tribe, and nation—is in need of re-creation. Not to know that, not to work at that, not to pray for that is to fail to be Christ's church.

Christian nurture is another indispensable part in the effort of God's people. "By tending the flock through the ministry of the Word and sacraments and through daily pastoral care" is the way we describe this aspect of the service which fulfills God's program.

How necessary this nurture is! Christian growth begins with birth, the divinely given new life which enables us to follow the call of Christ. But what feeding, what fellowship, and what care are necessary for the restoration to move from one stage of splendor to the next! God maintains his first creation; through the Word we are confronted with his love and his will; through the sacraments (or ordinances, if you prefer) he reminds us of Christ's life, death, and resurrection and calls for our loyalty; through pastoral cares he reproves our weakness, corrects our failures, care for our hurts.

The church is always on the way to restoration. One of her joys is to experience the constant renewal that Christ has offered in his word, his baptism, his table, and his shepherds.

Social concern is the third indispensable part in the efforts of God's people. We serve God, our Statement reminds us, "by striving for social justice and by relieving human distress and need." The care of the church can never be confined to her boundaries.

As part of God's new creation, she resents every vestige of the old order. The war, the bigotry, the oppression, the exploitation that are a way of life in a fallen world, the church hates. Because she—of all members of society—should know the toll sin takes and the changes God wants to bring, she must spend herself in deeds of justice and compassion.

The God whom we worship has shown himself to care deeply about justice and compassion and the people who are deprived of them. To what avail is our worship of God if his character has not rubbed off on us?

Our work is cut out for us. The world has all the marks of imminent collapse. The cry for renewal has never been stronger.

Christ, the master Architect of creation and history, is hard at it, making all things new. It is restoration and much more that he is working at. Christ's ultimate purpose will outshine even Eden's bliss. He it is who has summoned us to be the church, his church. His participation assures our success. The church can be confident of one thing: if the living Lord can make us new, if he can turn our idolatry to worship and our vagrancy to service, no task is too hard for him. That confidence gives us heart to renew our commitment. We want to be nothing less than all he has pledged himself to make us.

STATEMENT OF FAITH ARTICLE **10**

God's redemptive purpose will be consummated by the return of Christ to raise the dead, to judge all people according to the deeds done in the body, and to establish his glorious kingdom. The wicked shall be separated from God's presence, but the righteous, in glorious bodies, shall live and reign with him forever. Then shall the eager expectation of the creation be fulfilled and the whole earth shall proclaim the glory of the God who makes all things new.

SCRIPTURE

*This is now the second letter that I have written to you,
    beloved, and in both of them I have aroused your
        sincere mind by way of reminder;
that you should remember the predictions of the holy
    prophets and the commandment of the Lord and Savior
        through your apostles.
First of all you must understand this, that scoffers will come
    in the last days with scoffing, following their own
        passions and saying, "Where is the promise of his
        coming?
For ever since the fathers fell asleep, all things have
    continued as they were from the beginning of creation."
They deliberately ignore this fact, that by the word of God
    heavens existed long ago, and an earth formed out of
        water, through which the world that then existed
            was deluged with water and perished.
But by the same word the heavens and earth that now exist
    have been stored up for fire, being kept until the day of
        judgment and destruction of ungodly men.
But do not ignore this one fact, beloved, that with the Lord
    one day is as a thousand years, and a thousand years as
        one day.*

The Lord is not slow about his promise as some count
    slowness, but is forbearing toward you, not wishing that
    any should perish,
But the day of the Lord will come like a thief, and then the
    heavens will pass away with a loud noise, and the
        elements will be dissolved with fire,
        and the earth and the works that are upon it
        will be burned up.
Since all these things are thus to be dissolved, what sort of
    persons ought you to be
in lives of holiness and godliness, waiting for and hastening
    the coming of the day of God, because of which the
        heavens will be kindled and dissolved,
        and the elements will melt with fire!
But according to his promise we wait for new heavens and a
    new earth in which righteousness dwells.
                         II Peter 3:1-13

CHAPTER *10*

The Hope Toward Which We Look

It is the last of a chain of great surprises. It is the climax of a program in which God has startled creation and the human family time and again. The second coming of Jesus Christ is the surprise to end all surprises.

Think how surprised the angels must have been when the voice of God shattered the silence of eternity and spoke the worlds into being. Think how surprised Abraham must have been when God plucked him from his settled civilization in Ur and dispatched him on his pilgrim journey. And what about Moses' surprise when the voice at the bush called him from the quiet security of Midian and sent him back to face the turmoil of Pharaoh's court?

Or David's surprise, sheltered as he was from life's large responsibilities by an army of older brothers, when God anointed him for kingship. God's enemies, too, have felt the sting of his surprises. What a story Sennacherib could tell about the havoc God wrought on his Assyrian armies overnight, just when they were set to swamp Jerusalem in Hezekiah's day.

And the Bethlehem shepherds—they were expert witnesses to God's surprises as angels brightened the night with song and announced unprecedented joy to the world. Mary Magdalene also felt that surprise as she heard the mysterious figure, whom she thought to be the gardener, call her name in the dawn's pale light and turned to face the risen Christ.

Surprises have been God's way of working from beginning to end. The new, the startling, the unexpected are what he does. These surprises—doing new things and saying new words—are his chief way of creating hope in the hearts of his people.

Christ's second coming is the surprise to which all God's other surprises point. It is the overwhelming culmination of a plan at which he has been working since the beginning. It is the hope toward which he has been pointing his people during the forty centuries between Abraham's day and ours. All else that God has done has had that day in mind.

Some years ago, during the cold nights of October, the New York Yankees and the Cincinnati Reds battled for the world championship of baseball. The commissioner had signed a lucrative contract with the television networks who pay dearly for the privilege of showing the games in prime time. The fans, trying to keep warm, shrouded themselves in blankets. Infielders spent the night sneaking blue fingers into their hop pockets, hitters warming their bats with hot water bottles. Someone asked a Cincinnati mainstay how he felt about the frigid environment. He responded with a customary enthusiasm: "I don't care if it snows. Playing in the World Series is the reason why I went to spring training!"

Throughout the long season the team played all its 162 games with one goal in mind—winning the National League pennant in order to earn a crack at the world championship. It was that goal that determined everything else they did. Their life's program was dominated by that hope.

So it is with God and his people—only our hope is based upon the unshakeable Word of God. We are those who hope in an eternal fellowship with the Father, Son, and Holy Spirit, listeners of God who joy and love in what we have heard, the many who throughout the ages have tasted the goodness of God, whose names are strewn across the pages of the history of the great march of civilization. And all hold in common the great hope God in Christ has freely given our race.

Here are the words with which our Fuller Statement expresses that hope: "God's redemptive purpose will be consummated by the return of Christ to raise the dead, to judge all people according to the deeds done in the body, and to establish his glorious kingdom." Three bright facets of hope shine from these words: 1) the hope of Christ's return; 2) the hope of Christ's judgement; 3) the hope of Christ's renewal.

The hope of Christ's return

What is hope for those who wait for Christ's return is a surprise for those who do not wait. Theirs is the surprise of intervention. Whatever they think about history, they do not think that it will end this way. "All things will stay the same" is their motto. History seems but a treadmill on which for exercise the human family runs, an effort that cannot lead us beyond ourselves. Or we may see it as an endless conveyor belt carrying our contributions into the future for generations yet unborn to enjoy and in turn pass on to their posterity. Either way there is no thought of an ending. Christ's intervention will come as a surprise, a surprise that alters the secular reading of history—whether viewed with the pessimism of the treadmill or the optimism of the conveyor belt.

What is surprise for those who misunderstand God's purpose is hope for us Christians. Ours is the hope of consummation. We have been told by God himself where history is heading, and we long for that day of victory to come.

Christ's return means that God's purpose will be fulfilled. The long path that began outside a garden gate, when a dejected couple shuffled off into the lonely night, will reach its destination in the bright light that turns radiant the clouds of glory. The sword-wielding cherubim who once barred the way to the tree of life will be replaced by the archangel whose rousing shout will herald the King's return. The rescue operation will be completed; the restoration and recreation of the old edifice will reach its splendid finish. All that God set out to do to draw his wayward family back to him will have been done. The mystery of revelation and reconciliation, so often perceived only by the few, will be fully unveiled to the many. The lowly Jesus, despised and rejected of men, will be seen by all as the living Lord who "comes to make his glories known, far as the curse is found."

Christ's return also means that the dead will be raised. The Lord who returns is the Lord of life, himself risen from the dead. As his coming fulfills history's purpose, so it defeats creation's greatest enemy, the curse of death. Nowhere is his mission as the last Adam—God's true man—evidenced more clearly that in the final resurrection of the dead:

"For as by a man came death, by a man has come also the resurrection of the dead. For as in Adam all die, so also in Christ shall all be made alive" (I Corinthians 15:21-22). Adam's rebellion led to death the whole human family; Christ's obedience will lead to resurrection all of Adam's sons and daughters.

Resurrection means the end to divided existence. The long struggle—the psychosomatic battle—between our diseased, decaying, enfeebled bodies and our inner selves will be put behind us forever. "Keeping body and soul together" is the facetious way that we speak of sustaining life. But it is gloomy humor, because that is the real human contest this side of Adam's sin. We live at war within ourselves, and death always wins that war within ourselves, and death always wins by forcing the ultimate division of human personhood. We use the word "ultimate" because that is what it seems like when we lower a body into a grave. At that moment the permanence of death seems to have the upper hand. But we are moving toward resurrection—a reality which Christ's resurrection anticipates—and death is not ultimate but penultimate; not permanent but temporary. Wholeness will again be our human experience, thanks to God's power of resurrection which will be grandly displayed at Christ's return.

The hope of Christ's judgment

The King who comes is also our Judge. As the Creator who knows why he made us and as the Law-giver who gave us explicit demands, he holds our whole race accountable. Judgement is the necessary conclusion to creation. If we are accidents of biochemistry, who have no purpose beyond adaptation for survival, then judgment is nonsense. If, however, we are part of a plan, participants in a holy purpose, then judgment is a necessity.

For those who have not trusted Christ, judgment will come as a complete surprise—the surprise of exclusion. Evangelicals have not enjoyed this doctrine, but they cannot escape it. The Fuller Statement has tried to capture the biblical teaching, grim though it is: "The wicked shall be separated from God's presence, but the righteous, in glorious bodies, shall live and reign with him forever."

To be separated from God's presence—what a defeat for God's enemies! No grace, no life, no holiness, no goodness will be available to them. Everything that makes life pleasant and noble comes from God. Without his presence what can life offer but anguish, frustration, remorse, despair? No wonder the Bible calls that state of exclusion from God's presence "the second death."

Yet, despite its terror, this judgment is something that we can hope for. It will mark the end of conflict in God's universe, the end of opposition to God's program. That enmity which has been the context for all God's activities since Satan opposed him in the garden will be done away with. All the powers on earth, in heaven and in hell that have sought to block God's work of restoration will be put down, and God will reign alone as King. That is part of what judgment means.

If the judgment comes to unbelievers with strong surprise, we who have been granted grace to know and trust the living God wait for it with high hope—the hope of fellowship. In Jesus' death on the cross, we have already been judged. The Judge who wields history's final gavel holds it in a nail-pierced hand. The guilty verdict that was directed toward us called for our death as punishment. That death he died in our place. Our final judgment he bore that bleak Friday when the sun refused to shine. He was forsaken by the Father that we might have eternal fellowship as we "shall live and reign" with God forever. Final judgment means the reward of God's people.

Whatever else the final judgment may accomplish, it surely confirms the redeeming work of the cross. The division that the cross makes in human history is established for all eternity: those who met their judgment there by faith in Jesus do not meet it later; those who did not, face the certainty and permanence of judgment. What they chose on earth—to live apart from the loving God—will be their destiny eternally. They face a surprise of incalculable horror.

The hope of Christ's renewal

This judgment is a part of all God's renewal. It is the settling of old accounts to make way for the age of splendor, in which God's will is fully done on earth as it is in heaven.

The entire universe is God's creation, a marvelous expression of his own beauty and order. All of it—from the massive suns that brighten the countless galaxies to the minute particles and charges that energize the atom—all of it is made to reveal his glory. It is an interdependent system finely tuned to sing God's praise. Sing it did—with full voice and solid intonation. Then we sinned, we human rebels. And our sinning jarred the system.

Now it partly sings and partly groans. The heavens proclaim God's glory, yet the whole creation "waits with eager longing for the revealing of the sons of God; for the creation was subjected to futility, not of its own will but by the will of him who subjected it in hope; because the creation itself will be set free from its bondage to decay and obtain the glorious liberty of the children of God. We know that the whole creation has been groaning in travail together until now; and not only the creation, but we ourselves, who have the first fruits of the Spirit, groan inwardly as we wait for adoption as sons, the redemption of our bodies. For in this hope we were saved ... " (Romans 8:19-24).

What a picture of hope, so explosive that we stagger before it! The redemption of our bodies—the final resurrection—carries with it the renewal, the liberation, of all creation. No more decay, no more conflict, no more death. The law of entropy that points to the collapse of our universe is replaced by the law of renewal in the majestic thermodynamics of God's salvation. Thus in triumph our Fuller Statement concludes: "Then shall the eager expectation of the creation be fulfilled and the whole earth shall proclaim the glory of God who makes all things new."

It is for Christ's renewal that we hope as we wait for his day to come. In a sense it will not be a surprise. He has told us of its coming, and we believe him.

In another sense, it will be filled with surprises. Because God has promised, we can hope with full confidence. All that he has foretold will take place. Because God had promised, even what we hope for will be filled with surprise; the surprise that comes from seeing him, from being with him, from watching him make all things new—even us!